Should Marijuana Be Legalized?

Scott Barbour

ReferencePoint Press®

San Diego, CA

© 2011 ReferencePoint Press, Inc.

For more information, contact:
ReferencePoint Press, Inc.
PO Box 27779
San Diego, CA 92198
www.ReferencePointPress.com

Picture credits:
Cover: iStockphoto.com
Maury Aaseng: 31
AP Images: 17, 23, 38, 57, 62
iStockphoto.com: 12
Landov: 8, 35, 49, 71, 77
Photoshot: 27
Science Photo Library: 42

LIBRARY OF CONGRESS CATALOGING-IN-PUBLICATION DATA

Barbour, Scott, 1963–
  Should marijuana be legalized? / by Scott Barbour.
    p. cm. — (In controversy series)
  Includes bibliographical references and index.
  ISBN-13: 978-1-60152-106-4 (hardback : alk. paper)
  ISBN-10: 1-60152-106-5 (hardback : alk. paper) 1. Marijuana—Juvenile literature. 2. Marijuana abuse—Juvenile literature. 3. Marijuana—Law and legislation—United States—Juvenile literature. 4. Marijuana—Therapeutic use—United States—Juvenile literature. I. Title.
  HV5822.M3B37 2009
  344.7305'45—dc22
                                                    2009040002

Contents

Foreword

I n 2008, as the U.S. economy and economies worldwide were falling into the worst recession since the Great Depression, most Americans had difficulty comprehending the complexity, magnitude, and scope of what was happening. As is often the case with a complex, controversial issue such as this historic global economic recession, looking at the problem as a whole can be overwhelming and often does not lead to understanding. One way to better comprehend such a large issue or event is to break it into smaller parts. The intricacies of global economic recession may be difficult to understand, but one can gain insight by instead beginning with an individual contributing factor such as the real estate market. When examined through a narrower lens, complex issues become clearer and easier to evaluate.

This is the idea behind ReferencePoint Press's *In Controversy* series. The series examines the complex, controversial issues of the day by breaking them into smaller pieces. Rather than looking at the stem cell research debate as a whole, a title would examine an important aspect of the debate such as *Is Stem Cell Research Necessary?* or *Is Embryonic Stem Cell Research Ethical?* By studying the central issues of the debate individually, researchers gain a more solid and focused understanding of the topic as a whole.

Each book in the series provides a clear, insightful discussion of the issues, integrating facts and a variety of contrasting opinions for a solid, balanced perspective. Personal accounts and direct quotes from academic and professional experts, advocacy groups, politicians, and others enhance the narrative. Sidebars add depth to the discussion by expanding on important ideas and events. For quick reference, a list of key facts concludes every chapter. Source notes, an annotated organizations list, bibliography, and index provide student researchers with additional tools for papers and class discussion.

The *In Controversy* series also challenges students to think critically about issues, to improve their problem-solving skills, and to sharpen their ability to form educated opinions. As President Barack Obama stated in a March 2009 speech, success in the twenty-first century will not be measurable merely by students' ability to "fill in a bubble on a test but whether they possess 21st century skills like problem-solving and critical thinking and entrepreneurship and creativity." Those who possess these skills will have a strong foundation for whatever lies ahead.

No one can know for certain what sort of world awaits today's students. What we can assume, however, is that those who are inquisitive about a wide range of issues; open-minded to divergent views; aware of bias and opinion; and able to reason, reflect, and reconsider will be best prepared for the future. As the international development organization Oxfam notes, "Today's young people will grow up to be the citizens of the future: but what that future holds for them is uncertain. We can be quite confident, however, that they will be faced with decisions about a wide range of issues on which people have differing, contradictory views. If they are to develop as global citizens all young people should have the opportunity to engage with these controversial issues."

In Controversy helps today's students better prepare for tomorrow. An understanding of the complex issues that drive our world and the ability to think critically about them are essential components of contributing, competing, and succeeding in the twenty-first century.

Divided Opinions and Conflicting Values

O n January 31, 2009, the British tabloid *News of the World* published a photograph of Olympic swimmer Michael Phelps, the winner of a record 8 gold medals at the 2008 Summer Games, smoking marijuana through a bong at a party in South Carolina. Following the photo's publication, many people wondered how the incident would affect Phelps's career, especially his income from endorsements. The swimmer quickly issued a public apology, and in the end he lost only one sponsor, Kellogg's, while retaining sponsorship deals with Mazda, Subway, Speedo, and other companies. Summing up the impact of the controversy on Phelps's career, *Los Angeles Times* journalist Dan Neil said, "There were no serious consequences. . . . The bong-heard-round-the-world scandal might as well never have happened."[1]

Neil and others contend that the absence of a negative backlash against Phelps is due to the public's growing acceptance of marijuana and its possible legalization. Jill Porter, a columnist for the *Philadelphia Daily News*, writes, "The very fact that the Olympian athlete hasn't been deep-sixed by some of his sponsors shows how tolerant our society has become of the recreational use of weed." Indeed, statistics reveal that nearly half of adult Americans admit to having tried marijuana. Porter views this shift in attitude as a positive development: "Instead of forcing him from his pedestal, Phelps' recreational use of marijuana will no doubt push the pendulum further along the road to liberalization of pot laws. As well it should."[2]

Others view the Phelps incident in a less positive light. They concede that nearly half of Americans have tried marijuana; however, they point out, that means more than half have never touched the drug. Moreover, many are troubled by the idea that Phelps has become an unwitting poster boy for legalization. The editors of the *Florence (SC) Morning News* write: "For decades, a party wagon has been traversing America bent on loosening the country's moral standards. And now with Phelps at the reins, the thought that the wagon could be picking up steam is disturbing."[3]

Divided Opinions

Like the conflicting views of Porter and the *Florence Morning News*, polls reveal that American views on marijuana and its possible legalization are far from unanimous. An October 2009 Gallup poll found that 44 percent favor legalization, while 54 percent oppose it. Young adults appear more likely to support legalization than their elders: 52 percent of those under age 35 agreed that marijuana should be legal, whereas 36 percent of those aged 35 and older favored legalization.

The views of teens on the issue are also divided. According to the 2008 Monitoring the Future survey, an ongoing study of teens funded by the federal government, 59 percent said the use of marijuana should be either legal or a minor violation (like a traffic ticket) but not a crime; only 28 percent said it should be a crime. However, the same study found that large percentages of teens disapprove of marijuana use. Among twelfth graders, 67 percent disapprove of using marijuana occasionally, and 80 percent disapprove of using the drug regularly. These numbers were even higher among eighth and tenth graders. Thus, although teens appear to take a fairly liberal stance on the legalization of marijuana, many harbor strong personal beliefs against its use.

Shifting Views on Legalization

Middle-aged Americans also hold contradictory views on marijuana and legalization. Many in the baby boom generation (those

A photographer caught Olympic gold medalist Michael Phelps (shown here at the 2008 Beijing games) in the act of smoking marijuana. Reaction to the photo was mixed, reflecting the divided views Americans have toward marijuana.

born between 1945 and 1965) advocate legalization. Most boomers came of age in the 1960s, an era of relaxed values and drug experimentation. To many of this generation, the campaign for legalization is consistent with the traditional American value of individual freedom. Massachusetts representative Barney Frank, a strong advocate of marijuana legalization, expresses this view when he says, "I think John Stuart Mill had it right in the 1850s, when he argued that individuals should have the right to do what they want in private, so long as they don't hurt anyone else. It's a matter of personal liberty."[4]

Not everyone shares the view that the right to smoke marijuana is a matter of personal liberty, however. For example, although he favors legalizing marijuana, Scott Haig, an orthopedic surgeon, nevertheless disapproves of the drug: "There's something repulsive about the half-closed, red eyes—something that's selfish and irresponsible."[5] In fact, many critics contend that legalization, by encouraging such selfish behavior, would lead to various social problems, including increased drug use, higher health-care costs, and disrupted families. Responding to the argument that marijuana legalization is an issue of personal freedom, Barrett Duke, director of the Research Institute of the Ethics and Religious Liberty Commission of the Southern Baptist Convention, says, "Personal freedom must be tempered by personal and social responsibility."[6]

Indeed, many baby boomers are finding that their views on the issue change as they grow older and have children of their own. Michael Winerip, a journalist for the *New York Times*, writes that as a young man he enjoyed marijuana: "The 20-something me used marijuana in moderation, did not fall victim to reefer madness, [and] did not go on to harder drugs. . . . The 20-something me believed marijuana could be legalized, regulated and taxed like alcohol, providing much needed revenue." However, now that he is in his 50s, his attitude has changed: "The 50-something me, the parent of three boys and a girl, ages 14 to 21, is not so sure. The 50-something me— who hasn't smoked in more than 20 years—knows stories in our little suburb about classmates of my kids smoking pot in middle-school, using heroin in college, going into rehab, relapsing, trying again." This experience has led Winerip to take an ambiguous stance on the legalization of marijuana: "It may make sense. It may happen. But with so many boomers . . . [who are] now parents, I'm not so sure."[7]

Thus, a person's position on the legalization of marijuana depends on a variety of factors, including age, philosophical bent, and phase of life. Because opinions on the issue are so deeply rooted in personal values, it appears unlikely that consensus on the legalization of marijuana will occur anytime soon.

Facts

- An ABC/Washington Post poll from February 2009 found that 45 percent of baby boomers favored legalization of marijuana, compared with 30 percent of those over 65.

- According to the National Survey on Drug Use and Health, in 2007, 14.4 million Americans aged 12 or older used marijuana at least once in the month prior to being surveyed.

- The National Survey on Drug Use and Health found that about 6,000 people a day, or a total of 2.1 million Americans, used marijuana for the first time in 2007. Of these, 62.2 percent were under 18.

- According to the 2008 Monitoring the Future survey, 61 percent of twelfth graders say they would not use marijuana even if it were made legal, 16.4 percent say they would use it as often as or less often than they use it now, 5.5 percent say they would use it more often than they do now, and 8.9 percent say they would try it for the first time.

- According to the 2008 Monitoring the Future survey, 39 percent of twelfth-grade students believed that the use of marijuana in private should be prohibited by law.

CHAPTER ONE

What Are the Origins of the Marijuana Legalization Debate?

Marijuana, also known as cannabis, has been used as medicine since ancient times. Anthropologists have found evidence that marijuana was used in Assyria, China, India, Greece, Egypt, Persia, and other ancient civilizations for ritualistic purposes, pain relief, and the treatment of various ailments. In colonial America settlers cultivated marijuana, but they grew a variety of the plant that causes little or no intoxicating effect and is instead used to produce hemp, a type of fiber used for textiles such as paper, fabric, and rope.

Doctors around the world used marijuana, or a processed form of the drug known as hashish, throughout the nineteenth century for providing patients with pain relief. Prior to the arrival of aspirin late in the century, marijuana was the most commonly used painkiller. In Britain doctors prescribed it as an appetite stimulant, pain reliever, and muscle relaxant as well as a treatment for seizures and insomnia. According to Madelon Lubin Finkel, a professor of clinical public health at Cornell University, "Marijuana and hashish extracts were the most prescribed medicines in the United

States [in the nineteenth century], and in 1870, cannabis was listed as a medicine in the *U.S. Pharmacopoeia*,"[8] the official registry of medications approved for use in the United States. However, she notes, by the end of the century, the use of marijuana had declined as doctors disputed the usefulness of the drug compared with other medicines.

The Beginnings of Federal Drug Control

In the early twentieth century, a large number of Americans were addicted to drugs. Many of them were white, rural women who had become hooked on morphine found in patent medicines, unregulated products of dubious quality that were widely available at the time. In response to this problem, the federal government began passing legislation to control the importation, production, and distribution of narcotics. The Pure Food and Drug Act of 1906 required that the contents of medicines be clearly labeled, effectively killing the patent medicine industry.

The leafy, green marijuana plant has found many uses over the years. It has been used to relieve pain, to stimulate appetite, and to get high. Some varieties of marijuana have also been grown for use in textiles such as paper, fabric, and rope.

Following passage of the Pure Food and Drug Act, federal laws were aimed less at hapless victims of quack doctors and more at the perceived threat posed by willing addicts, especially immigrants and minorities. Wendy Chapkis, a professor of sociology and women and gender studies at the University of Southern Maine, and Richard J. Webb, a lecturer in communications studies at San Jose State University, explain:

> While addiction of the nineteenth century might have been largely a white and female problem, concern about the use of addictive substances quickly became focused on the danger of their use by racial minorities and immigrants. The result was a shift in approach to drug regulation. . . . Early federal drug regulations were justified, then, on the grounds that they served to protect the public from drug-crazed minorities and accidental addicts.[9]

To this end, Congress passed several laws aimed at keeping narcotics out of the hands of the public. These included the Harrison Narcotic Act of 1914, which granted the federal government the authority to tax and regulate the sale and distribution of narcotics; the Jones-Miller Act of 1922, which imposed stiff penalties for the importation of narcotics; and the Narcotic Drug Import and Export Act of 1922, which sought to end the illegitimate use of narcotics. These early federal drug laws were not aimed specifically at marijuana, but they established the regulatory framework under which marijuana would eventually be controlled.

"Early federal drug regulations were justified ... on the grounds that they served to protect the public from drug-crazed minorities and accidental addicts."[9]

— Wendy Chapkis, a professor of sociology and women and gender studies at the University of Southern Maine, and Richard J. Webb, a lecturer in communications studies at San Jose State University.

State Laws Against Marijuana

As the federal government began to regulate narcotics, states enacted their own laws specifically targeted at marijuana, beginning with Utah in 1915. Some southwestern and Rocky Mountain states, such as Texas, New Mexico, Montana, and Colorado, passed laws in response to the sudden arrival of the drug in the hands of Mexican migrant workers. Others, including California, Washington, Oregon, and New York, created their laws to prevent an

What Is Marijuana?

Marijuana, or cannabis, is a drug that comes from the plant *Cannabis sativa*. The plant's leaves and flowers contain the chemical delta-9-tetrahydrocannabinol, or THC. Although its effects can vary depending on the person and the setting in which the drug is taken, most people who smoke or ingest THC experience a euphoric state commonly referred to as being "high" or "stoned." The flowers (most commonly known as buds) contain the highest concentration of THC and are therefore the most valuable part of the plant. The raw plant is sometimes processed into a concentrated resinous substance known as hashish. This form of the drug is most commonly found in Central Asia and North Africa. Marijuana is usually smoked in a cigarette (commonly known as a joint), a pipe, or a water pipe known as a bong. It is also sometimes smoked in a cigar that has been emptied of tobacco and refilled with marijuana (known as a blunt). Besides being smoked, marijuana is often mixed in food or teas or converted to a vapor that is inhaled.

increase in the use of marijuana as a substitute for alcohol, which was outlawed by the Eighteenth Amendment in 1919, as well as for opium, heroin, and cocaine, which were becoming increasingly hard to obtain due to the passage of federal drug laws. In all, 27 states passed laws against the use of marijuana prior to the 1930s.

The Marijuana Tax Act of 1937

In the early 1930s the federal government began an effort to include marijuana along with opium, heroin, and cocaine in its scope of regulatory control. This effort was led by Harry J. Anslinger, the head of the Federal Bureau of Narcotics, the government agency responsible for drug control at the time. Anslinger was convinced that marijuana posed a serious threat to society. He advocated passage of a new federal law, the Marijuana Tax Act of 1937. During congressional hearings about the legislation, Anslinger offered testimony in which he claimed the drug was harmful and had no medical use:

> Some individuals have a complete loss of sense of time or a sense of value. They lose their sense of place. They have an increased feeling of physical strength and power. Some people will fly into a delirious rage, and they are temporarily irresponsible and may commit violent crimes. Other people will laugh uncontrollably. . . . It is dangerous to the mind and body, and particularly dangerous to the criminal type, because it releases all of the inhibitions.[10]

In opposition to Anslinger, the American Medical Association (AMA), the nation's most prestigious medical professional organization, opposed passage of the Marijuana Tax Act. William C. Woodward, the legislative counsel of the AMA, testified before Congress that while the use of marijuana for medical purposes had declined, more research might lead to the discovery of the drug's health benefits: "To say, . . . as has been proposed here, that the use of the drug should be prevented by a prohibitive tax, loses sight of the fact that future investigation may show that there are substantial medical uses for Cannabis."[11]

Despite Woodward's efforts, the Marijuana Tax Act of 1937 was passed into law. The new regulation did not completely outlaw marijuana. However, it banned the importation of cannabis into the United States and placed heavy taxes on marijuana dealers and transactions. Although the 1937 law did not significantly reduce marijuana use, it represented a shift in how the drug was perceived in the United States. As Chapkis and Webb put it, marijuana had gone "from widely used medicine to increasingly regulated substance to dangerous—and prohibited—drug."[12]

More Federal Control

The Marijuana Tax Act of 1937 did little to stop the use of marijuana. However, Anslinger continued his crusade against the drug.

Due primarily to his efforts, in 1941 marijuana was struck from the *U.S. Pharmacopoeia*. In addition, in 1961 the United States signed on to the Single Convention on Narcotic Drugs, a United Nations (UN) treaty that made marijuana and its cultivation illegal around the globe.

Despite the government's ongoing clampdown on marijuana, use of the drug increased in the 1960s. Whereas in past decades marijuana had been associated with minorities, the inner-city poor, and the beatniks of the 1950s, in the 1960s the drug spread into the white mainstream, primarily due to the counterculture movement. As described by journalists Charles Cooper and Declan McCullagh: "When the youth counterculture emerged in the 1960s, its embrace of drugs forced lawmakers and police to deal with a sudden demographic change: Marijuana was no longer a problem confined to Hispanics and blacks. The sons and daughters of the white middle class were also toking up, and in significant numbers."[13]

In response to this perceived problem, in 1970 the federal government established the National Commission on Marijuana and Drug Abuse to study the harms of marijuana use. However, the commission reached conclusions that contradicted the government's stance. It found that marijuana posed few risks and recommended that possession of small amounts of the drug for personal use be decriminalized. Because these findings ran contrary to the position of the federal government, they were rejected. Instead of decriminalizing marijuana, President Richard Nixon declared a "war on drugs," a large-scale effort to fight drug trafficking, possession, and use by means of tough laws and police tactics.

As part of the war on drugs, in 1970 Congress passed the Comprehensive Drug Abuse Prevention and Control Act (commonly known as the Controlled Substances Act). This law repealed the Marijuana Tax Act and combined over 50 laws into one regulatory scheme in which marijuana was grouped with other illegal narcotics such as cocaine and heroin. In addition, it set up a system in which each drug was assigned to 1 of 5 "schedules" depending on its medical properties and potential for

"If there is any future for marijuana as a medicine, it lies in its isolated components, the cannabinoids [active chemicals of marijuana] and their synthetic derivatives. Isolated cannabinoids will provide more reliable effects than crude plant mixtures."[17]

— Institute of Medicine, an independent, nonprofit research organization.

addiction. Marijuana was declared a Schedule I drug, meaning it had no medical use but a high potential for abuse. In this classification marijuana could not be prescribed by a doctor except as part of government-approved research. By comparison, morphine and cocaine were declared Schedule II drugs, which meant that despite their potential for abuse, they were deemed to have medical use and could be prescribed by doctors.

The Movement for Legalization

In response to the federal government's hard-line stance against the drug, activists began to lobby for the liberalization of the nation's marijuana laws. The National Organization for the Reform of Marijuana Laws (NORML) was formed in 1970, the same year as the passage of the Controlled Substances Act, with the goal of legalizing marijuana. Partly as a result of NORML's efforts, 11 states passed laws to decriminalize marijuana. *Decriminalization* does not mean outright legalization; rather, it typically means that the possession and use of a small amount of marijuana is a civil offense similar to a traffic violation, rather than a misdemeanor or felony criminal offense. Growing, selling, or possessing large amounts of cannabis remains illegal in states that have decriminalized the drug.

The Beginning of the Medical Marijuana Movement

Although the federal government effectively blocked most research into the medical uses of marijuana, people began to learn about the drug's potential health benefits. Anecdotal evidence suggested that the drug might be useful for treating pain, reducing the eye pressure that can cause blindness in people with glaucoma, alleviating muscle spasms and tics due to multiple sclerosis, and easing nausea and vomiting, especially in patients undergoing chemotherapy for cancer. According to Finkel, "As word [of these medical benefits of cannabis] spread, many more individuals started self-medicating with marijuana."[14]

One such individual, Robert Randall, was arrested for cultivating marijuana for use as medicine. He defended himself in federal court by using a little-known doctrine called the "necessity defense," arguing that he needed the drug as treatment for his glaucoma. In 1976 Judge James Washington not only acquitted Randall of all charges but required the federal government to supply him with marijuana. To comply with the ruling, the government established the Compassionate Investigational New Drug Program, which grew marijuana for Randall under the supervision of the National Institute on Drug Abuse. However, the creation of this program proved to be an anomaly rather than a shift in the nation's drug policy toward legalization. While other patients received marijuana through the program, the number was never larger than 30 at any time, and the program was closed to new entrants in 1991.

The Legalization Movement in the 1980s

During the 1980s the federal government continued its hard-line stance against marijuana for both recreational and medical purposes. It passed a series of laws that stiffened the penalties for marijuana possession, trafficking, and distribution. At the same time, proponents of legalization of marijuana continued to press for legalization. NORML, now joined by the Alliance for Cannabis Therapeutics, an organization seeking legalization of marijuana for medical purposes, demanded public hearings on the rescheduling of marijuana. In 1986 the U.S. Drug Enforcement Administration (DEA) held

Reefer Madness

In 1936 a church group financed a movie titled *Tell Your Children*, which was intended to teach parents about the dangers marijuana posed to their children. The film depicts a sequence of tragic events that result when several high school students are lured into using marijuana by a local drug pusher. High on marijuana, characters in the film go insane and commit murder, rape, and suicide. While the film did not reach a wide audience at the time of its release, in the 1970s it was rediscovered. Billed under a new title, *Reefer Madness*, it became a cult classic among marijuana smokers, who found it funny due to its overacting, its heavy-handed moralistic message, and its wildly inaccurate portrayal of the effects of marijuana. For example, after smoking marijuana, characters are depicted as being hyperactive, whereas marijuana has the opposite effect. Marijuana impairs users' ability to think clearly and remember, impedes hand-eye coordination, and slows reaction time, but it does not typically cause users to go criminally insane. The film has become such an icon of American popular culture that the phrase "reefer madness" is commonly used as shorthand for overblown hysteria about the harms of marijuana use.

hearings on the issue, at which Randall and many other proponents of medical marijuana submitted testimony.

In 1988 DEA administrative law judge Francis L. Young concluded that marijuana was safe and effective when used by a doctor to treat muscle spasms and nausea resulting from chemotherapy. He further stated that to reach any other conclusion on the issue "would be unreasonable, arbitrary, and capricious."[15] Despite this ruling by a high official within its own agency, the DEA refused to alter its stance on marijuana, and the drug remains a Schedule I substance today.

State Medical Marijuana Initiatives

The clash between the federal government and legalization advocates continued into the 1990s. Unable to influence the federal government, the legalization movement turned to the state initiative process. In 1996 Arizona and California became the first 2 states to pass voter initiatives legalizing marijuana for medical purposes. Arizona's Proposition 200 required patients to obtain a doctor's prescription. Because marijuana is a Schedule I drug, it is illegal for physicians to prescribe it; therefore, the Arizona law was merely symbolic and had no practical effect.

California's Proposition 215, also known as the Compassionate Use Act, avoided the flaws of the Arizona law by allowing doctors to recommend rather than prescribe the drug. It legalized the cultivation, possession, and use of marijuana when recommended by a physician. Since 1996 voters have approved initiatives legalizing medical marijuana in 8 other states: Alaska, Colorado, Maine, Michigan, Montana, Nevada, Oregon, and Washington. In addition, state legislatures have passed similar laws in 5 states: Hawaii, New Jersey, New Mexico, Rhode Island, and Vermont. In all, 14 states passed laws that protected both doctor and patient from prosecution under state marijuana laws when the doctor deemed marijuana to be an appropriate medication. (The legislature of a fifteenth state, Maryland, passed a medical marijuana law in 2003. However, this law only partially legalizes medical marijuana; it allows patients to be fined, although not jailed.)

Although 14 states legalized marijuana as medicine, the drug remained illegal under federal law. In response to state-level legalization, the federal government announced that it would revoke the medical license of any doctor who recommended marijuana to a patient. As Finkel puts it, "The federal government's stance was that the [state medical marijuana] propositions didn't change anything."[16]

The Institute of Medicine Report

In the face of this growing divide between state and federal policies on marijuana, in 1997 the federal government asked the Institute of Medicine (IOM), an independent, neutral, nonprofit research organization, to conduct a review of the research on the medical uses of marijuana. The IOM report, released in 1999, remains the definitive assessment of the potential harms and benefits of marijuana as medicine. However, far from settling the debate, the report gave some support to both sides. It concluded that smoking marijuana did have medical benefits for relieving pain, controlling nausea and vomiting induced by chemotherapy, and stimulating appetite in AIDS patients. Moreover, it concluded that the side effects of marijuana were no worse than those of other medications and that there was no evidence that allowing medical marijuana would lead to an increase in the use of other drugs.

On the other hand, the IOM pointed out that the hazards of smoking marijuana were similar to those of smoking tobacco: lung damage, harm to fetuses, and possibly cancer. It concluded that the medically beneficial chemicals in marijuana should be isolated and made available to patients in a nonsmoked form:

"Our federalist system, properly understood, allows California and a growing number of other States to decide for themselves how to safeguard the health and welfare of their citizens."[18]

— Clarence Thomas, associate justice of the U.S. Supreme Court.

> If there is any future for marijuana as a medicine, it lies in its isolated components, the cannabinoids [active chemicals of marijuana] and their synthetic derivatives. Isolated cannabinoids will provide more reliable effects than crude plant mixtures. Therefore, the purpose of clinical trials of smoked marijuana would not be to develop marijuana as a licensed drug but rather to serve as a first step toward the development of a nonsmoked rapid-onset cannabinoid delivery system.[17]

Opponents of marijuana legalization seized on this portion of the IOM report as confirmation that marijuana should not be approved as medicine.

The Supreme Court Rules on Medical Marijuana

The IOM report did little to quell the debate over the legal status of medical marijuana. The federal government maintained its stance that marijuana was a Schedule I substance and illegal under federal law. Meanwhile, citizens of California and other states with medical marijuana laws cultivated and used the drug under the supervision of the doctors who were willing to risk the sanction of the federal government. In response, the federal government routinely raided medical marijuana farms and arrested growers and distributors of the drug.

The Supreme Court took up the issue of medical marijuana in the early years of the twenty-first century. In 2001 in *U.S. v. Oakland Cannabis Buyers' Cooperative*, the Court ruled 8-0 (with one justice recusing himself from the case) that the medical necessity defense (the defense previously used by Randall) does not protect marijuana distributors from prosecution under federal drug laws. This ruling was limited to marijuana distributors (not medical patients) and did not overturn state laws allowing authorized patients to cultivate marijuana for their personal use or to possess and use marijuana regardless of how they obtained the drug.

In 2003 the Supreme Court again affected the medical marijuana issue by choosing not to hear an appeal in the case of *Conant v. Walters*. In *Conant* a lower court had ruled that preventing physicians from recommending marijuana to their patients was a violation of their First Amendment right to free speech. By refusing to entertain an appeal, the Supreme Court essentially upheld that decision, thereby protecting doctors who recommend marijuana from prosecution under federal law.

In 2005 the Court again ruled on the issue. In *Gonzales v. Raich* the Court ruled 6-3 that under the Commerce Clause of the U.S. Constitution, the federal government has jurisdiction over interstate commerce. Therefore, the Controlled Substances Act, which bans the cultivation and use of marijuana, overrides any state laws legalizing the drug, even for purely medical purposes. In

Angel Raich checks the marijuana buds that she uses for relieving chronic pain and the symptoms of an inoperable brain tumor. The U.S. Supreme Court ruled that Raich and others like her are not immune from federal prosecution on drug charges.

short the Court declared that state marijuana laws do not protect medical marijuana users from arrest and prosecution under federal law. Like *U.S. v. Oakland Cannabis Buyers' Cooperative*, *Gonzales v. Raich* did not overturn state laws legalizing marijuana for medical purposes, nor did it prevent additional states from passing such laws. It merely stated that federal officials can enforce federal laws even in states with medical marijuana laws.

The Court's decision in *Gonzales v. Raich* was far from unanimous. Three justices dissented on the grounds that, under the nation's federalist system, states had the right to establish their own commerce policies for trade within their borders. As stated by Justice Clarence Thomas, "Our federalist system, properly understood, allows California and a growing number of other States to decide for themselves how to safeguard the health and welfare of their citizens."[18] Thus, conflict within the Court reflected the larger conflict in society over the legal status of marijuana.

The Marijuana Legalization Debate Today

In the wake of *Raich*, the federal government maintained its stance in opposition to marijuana for both medical and recreational use. Authorities continued to raid dispensaries and arrest users in states with medical marijuana laws. However, various developments in 2009 seemed to give impetus to the legalization movement. The newly elected president, Barack Obama, acknowledged that he had smoked marijuana in his youth. (An earlier president, Bill Clinton, admitted he had tried marijuana but insisted he had not inhaled the smoke.) In addition, with the nation in a severe recession, many commentators argued that marijuana should be legalized and taxed to offset budget deficits. In May 2009 California governor Arnold Schwarzenegger created headlines when he publicly stated that this idea should be discussed. Finally, in October, the U.S. Department of Justice directed federal officials not to prosecute medical marijuana users and suppliers who were in compliance with state laws.

Perhaps as a result of these signals from government officials, public support for marijuana legalization has risen. According to a July 2009 CBS News poll, 41 percent of Americans favor legalization, up from 31 percent in March 2009. Other polls have returned even higher numbers. Cooper and Mc-Cullagh write that these developments suggest that marijuana legalization may be at hand:

> *"Legalization is not in the president's vocabulary, and it's not in mine."*[20]
>
> — Gil Kerlikowske, President Obama's director of the White House Office of National Drug Control Policy.

Today the potent smell of marijuana legalization is in the air. States including California and New Mexico . . . already permit marijuana's use for medicinal purposes. The success of those initiatives, coupled with an economic downturn, a president who did inhale and governors who are willing to discuss complete legalization, make it seem possible that legal bans on recreational use of marijuana will, in the not-so-distant future, go up in smoke.[19]

However, Cooper and McCullagh's prediction may be premature. In July 2009 Gil Kerlikowske, the director of the White House Office of National Drug Control Policy (ONDCP), announced that the federal government had no intention of changing its marijuana laws. He stated flatly: "Legalization is not in the president's vocabulary, and it's not in mine."[20] At the same time, raids of California's medical marijuana dispensaries continued, although at a slower pace. Moreover, the same poll that found 41 percent of Americans were in favor of legalization also found that 52 percent were opposed. Thus, while the tide of public and political opinion may have shifted slightly toward the legalization of marijuana, the debate over this controversial issue is far from settled.

Facts

- A 2007 Zogby poll found that only 24 percent of Americans believed that the nation's Founding Fathers would have approved of laws banning the use of marijuana.

- According to several Gallup polls, American public support for marijuana legalization rose from 12 percent in 1969 to 28 percent in 1977 and to 36 percent in 2005.

- In 1970 the U.S. government reported that 20 million Americans had smoked marijuana at least once. In 2005 that number was more than 112 million.

- According to the Substance Abuse and Mental Health Services Administration, more than 50.8 percent of men report that they have used marijuana at least once; that number is 41.6 percent among women.

- About 20 percent of Americans between the ages of 12 and 17 report that they have used marijuana in the past year. About 14 percent of adults have used the drug in the past year.

CHAPTER TWO

How Should Marijuana Laws Be Reformed?

Some people use marijuana to ease their pain and treat their illnesses. Others use it simply to enjoy its mood-altering effects. Laws have been passed to regulate both of these uses of the drug. Those who advocate legalization favor easing or overturning laws against the possession and use of marijuana for recreational use, medical use, or both. In general most proposals for legalization fall into one of three categories: decriminalization for recreational use, legalization for recreational use, or legalization for medical use. In opposition to these three choices is the option to keep marijuana illegal for both recreational and medical purposes; this is the option preferred by the federal government.

Decriminalization for Recreational Use

What is often called "legalization" of marijuana is really decriminalization. Whereas *legalization* means ending all legal prohibitions against the drug, *decriminalization* means easing the penalties associated with the drug's possession and use. Typically, in jurisdictions where marijuana has been decriminalized, possession of a small amount of the drug for personal use is either a misdemeanor or a civil penalty similar to a traffic ticket and subject to a relatively small fine but no jail time. However, cultivating, selling, and possessing large amounts of the drug remain felonies that can result in arrest and prison.

In the United States 13 states have decriminalized marijuana for nonmedical use. These states are Alaska, California, Colorado,

Maine, Massachusetts, Minnesota, Mississippi, Nebraska, Nevada, New York, North Carolina, Ohio, and Oregon. For example, in Oregon, the first state to decriminalize marijuana (in 1973) for recreational use, possessing less than 1 ounce (28.35g) of marijuana or cultivating less than 0.18 ounces (5g) of the drug is a misdemeanor punishable by a fine of $500 to $1,000 but no jail time. However, possessing or cultivating more than an ounce is a class B felony punishable by 10 years in prison and a fine of $100,000.

New York is even more lenient on possession of small amounts of marijuana. There, possessing up to 0.88 ounces (25g) is a civil offense punishable by a fine of from $100 for a first offense to $200 for a second offense. Possession of between 0.88 and 2 ounces (25 and 56.7 g) is a misdemeanor punishable by 3 months in jail and a $500 fine. The punishment increases for possession of larger amounts and for cultivation and sale of the drug.

In contrast, in states that have not decriminalized marijuana, possession and sale of the drug are more harshly punished. For example, in Tennessee, the possession, delivery, or sale of up to one-half ounce (14.2g) is a misdemeanor punishable by up to one year in jail and a fine of up to $2,500. Similarly, in Kansas, possession of any amount of the drug is punishable by one year in jail and a fine of $2,500.

Advocates of marijuana legalization march in New York in 2009. Some of the protestors urged legalization for medical purposes while others called for legalization for recreational use. Both are the subject of debate in cities and states around the nation.

Along with the 13 states that have decriminalized marijuana, many city governments have passed resolutions relaxing the enforcement of marijuana laws. In most cases these ordinances do not alter the sentencing guidelines; they simply state that the enforcement of marijuana laws will be a low priority within a particular city. For example, in 2003 voters in Seattle, Washington, approved Initiative 75, which made the arrest and prosecution of adults in possession of marijuana for personal use the lowest law-enforcement priority. More recently, voters in both Missoula, Montana (2006), and Denver, Colorado (2007), passed similar laws, known as Initiative 2 in Missoula and Question 100 in Denver. Berkeley, California, and Madison, Wisconsin, are among the other American cities that have voted to make marijuana enforcement a low priority.

The Rationale for Decriminalization

Advocates of decriminalization for recreational use contend that the economic costs of criminalizing marijuana outweigh the harms of the drug. An adult possessing a small amount of cannabis for personal use poses few risks to society, they insist. On the other hand, arresting and incarcerating that person imposes a large burden on society in terms of law enforcement and imprisonment costs. In addition, a felony conviction can cause irreparable harm to the career and family of a person arrested on a marijuana charge. According to the FBI, police made 847,863 arrests on marijuana charges in 2008. Of these, 89 percent were for possession, and only 11 percent were for sale or manufacture. The National Organization for the Reform of Marijuana Laws (NORML) sums up the argument for decriminalization:

> Marijuana prohibition needlessly destroys the lives and careers of literally hundreds of thousands of good, hardworking, productive citizens each year in this country. This is a misapplication of the criminal sanction that . . . wastes valuable law enforcement resources that should be focused on serious and violent crime.[21]

Beyond the cost-benefit argument for decriminalization, civil libertarians contend that adults should have the right to choose for themselves whether to smoke marijuana without the government intruding into their personal lives. Massachusetts representative Barney Frank expresses this view when he says, "I don't think it is the government's business to tell you how to spend your leisure time."[22] Will Wilkinson, a senior fellow at the Cato Institute, a libertarian public policy research organization, argues that marijuana should be legal in part because smoking it is enjoyable. "Pleasure matters too," he writes. "That's probably why Barack Obama smoked up the second and third times: because he liked it. That's why tens of millions of Americans regularly take a puff, despite the misconceived laws meant to save us from our own wickedness."[23]

Opponents of decriminalization counter that marijuana is far from a harmless drug and that penalties against its possession and use should remain strict. Chief among their concerns is that relaxing

Teens and Marijuana

Each year, researchers at the University of Michigan survey 50,000 teenagers in grades 8, 10, and 12 about their experiences with drugs, including marijuana. In 2008 this study, known as the Monitoring the Future (MTF) survey, found that 43 percent of twelfth graders report that they have tried marijuana at least once in their life. This number was up 1 percentage point from the previous year. However, the MTF researchers note that it was considerably lower than in 1999, when it reached 50 percent, and dramatically lower than 1980, when it reached a high of 60 percent. Thus, overall, the trend in teen marijuana use over the past 3 decades has been a decline. The MTF also found that laws against marijuana do little to keep the drug out of the hands of teens. In 2008, 84 percent of twelfth graders said marijuana was "fairly easy" or "very easy" to get.

marijuana laws for adults sends a dangerous and misguided signal to society that the drug is benign, leading to more marijuana use by young people. The editors of the *Christian Science Monitor*, a daily newspaper that strongly opposes the legalization of marijuana, argue that parents must resist the latest push to ease the nation's marijuana laws:

> Do parents really want marijuana to become a normal part of society—and an expectation for their children? . . . They must let lawmakers know that legalization is not OK, and they must carry this message to their children, too. . . . They need to teach the life lesson that marijuana does not really solve personal challenges, be they stress, relationships, or discouragement. In the same way, a search for joy and satisfaction in a drug is misplaced.[24]

Decriminalization on a National Scale?

Proponents of legalization advocate decriminalizing the drug on a national level. To this end, Frank introduced legislation in 2008 and 2009 to end federal penalties against adults caught in possession of fewer than 3.53 ounces (100g) of the drug. Under current federal law, the penalty for the possession of a small amount of marijuana for personal use is one year in prison and a $1,000 fine. The new law would remove these sanctions and leave marijuana enforcement up to the states, allowing each state either to retain or repeal its current marijuana laws.

Most commentators agree that Frank's bill has little chance of passing in Congress. However, if it were to pass, the United States would not be the first country to decriminalize marijuana. In recent years a growing number of nations have eased their marijuana laws, especially in Europe and Latin America. Thus far, the only European country with a stated policy of decriminalization is Portugal. In 2001 that country passed a law decriminalizing all drugs, including marijuana, heroin, and cocaine. Drugs remain illegal, and trafficking and selling drugs remain serious crimes. However, the possession or use of a small quantity of drugs (an amount needed for 10 days of personal use) is considered an administrative offense

Marijuana Laws by State

As of 2010, 13 U.S. states had decriminalized marijuana for nonmedical, recreational use. In these states possession of a small amount of marijuana, usually an ounce or less, is considered a misdemeanor or civil offense most often punishable by a fine. Fourteen states had also legalized marijuana for medical purposes as of 2010. In each of these states, patients may legally possess and use marijuana if recommended by a doctor; most states allow patients to grow marijuana as well. In one other state, Maryland, possession and use of marijuana for medical purposes does not carry jail time but can lead to a fine.

- Decriminalized for recreational purposes only
- Legalized for medical purposes only
- Legalized for medical use and decriminalized for recreational purposes
- Reduced penalties for medical marijuana

Sources: ProCon.org, "13 Legal Medical Marijuana States: Laws, Fees, and Possession Limits," 2009. http://medicalmarijuana.procon.org; Norml, "State by State Laws," 2008. http://norml.com.

rather than a criminal offense. Instead of being sent to jail, those in violation of the law are brought before a Dissuasion Commission, a 3-person panel consisting of a legal official and at least one person with a medical background, such as a doctor or social worker. The commission can recommend (but not require) drug abuse treatment, charge a fine, issue a warning, or impose no punishment.

In addition to Portugal and other countries in Europe, some Latin American nations are also softening their drug laws, including Uruguay, Paraguay, and Mexico. In April 2009 the Mexican government passed a law decriminalizing possession of small amounts of all drugs, including marijuana, heroin, cocaine, and methamphetamine. Under the new law, persons caught in possession of 0.18 ounces (5g) or less of marijuana will not be arrested but will instead be encouraged to seek treatment. After the third offense, treatment becomes mandatory.

Legalization for Recreational Use

While some advocate following the lead of Portugal, Mexico, and other countries that have decriminalized marijuana on a national scale, others promote full-scale legalization—that is, the removal of both civil and criminal penalties for the possession and use of marijuana for personal recreational use. Proponents of this view generally call for marijuana to be legalized, regulated, and taxed in a manner similar to alcohol and tobacco. However, it is not clear exactly how such a system would work. Would marijuana be available at the local market like alcohol and tobacco? Would it be advertised in magazines, on the radio, and on television? These questions are typically left unanswered in favor of more generalized statements of policy. For example, NORML's policy statement says, "A legally regulated market should be established where consumers could buy marijuana in a safe and secure environment."[25] Left unstated is what the "safe and secure environment" would be and how it would be regulated. Similarly, the mission statement of the Marijuana Policy Project calls for "a nation where marijuana is legally regulated similarly to alcohol."[26] Again, it is unclear how such regulation would be instituted.

One possible example for the logistics of legalization is the Netherlands. No country has completely legalized marijuana, but the Netherlands's policy comes closest to legalization. Although marijuana remains illegal, adults are permitted to buy small amounts of the drug and smoke it in specially licensed coffee shops. This policy is sometimes called de facto legalization,

"Do parents really want marijuana to become a normal part of society—and an expectation for their children?"[24]

— *Christian Science Monitor*, a national newspaper.

meaning it is legalization in practice. Supporters contend that this system of cannabis outlets could serve as a model for the regulated sale of marijuana in the United States.

Legalization Versus Prohibition

One of the main arguments for legalization is that the prohibition of marijuana causes more damage than the drug itself. Proponents of legalization contend that keeping the drug illegal has created an underground black market, driven up the price of the drug, and provided a lucrative source of income for international drug

Cannabis in Canada

As in the United States, a movement has emerged to de-criminalize marijuana in Canada. The drug is already legal for medical purposes, and advocates are pushing for broader liberalization of marijuana laws. Some argue that the drug is widely tolerated. They point to a 2007 UN study that found 17 percent of Canadians had used marijuana in the past year, a number more than 4 times the global average of 4 percent and the highest in the industrialized world (the U.S. past-year rate is about 11 percent). In addition, a 2008 poll by the polling company Angus Reid found that 53 percent of Canadians favor legalization of marijuana (most U.S. polls find rates of about 40 to 45 percent). Thus, momentum appears to be moving toward full legalization. However, not everyone agrees that Canada is overwhelmingly tolerant of marijuana. One professor suggests that as many as 71 percent of Canadians disapprove of its use. As stated by Charlie Gillis of *Maclean's* magazine, "Canada's overall attitude toward marijuana may not so much be one of openness as grudging acceptance: I can't stop you from smoking it, the message seems to be, but I'd rather you didn't."

Charlie Gillis, "Thank You for Not Smoking Up: Canada's Drift Toward Legalizing Pot May Be Coming to a Halt," *Maclean's*, August 25, 2008, p. 18.

cartels and other criminals who are willing to risk punishment in order to make a profit. America's antidrug effort, commonly referred to as the war on drugs, has failed to respond effectively to the problem, critics insist. The federal government alone spends more than $14 billion a year in an effort to stem drug trafficking, arrest and prosecute drug violators, and prevent substance abuse. However, drugs remain readily available and widely used. In fact, the rate of marijuana use in the United States is more than twice as high as nations with much less stringent drug policies, such as Portugal and the Netherlands.

Legalizing the drug, proponents contend, would spell an end to the drug cartels. Bringing the drug trade above ground would drive down the price of the drug and eliminate the incentive for criminal gangs to get involved in smuggling and dealing. Moreover, it would allow the government to oversee safety and regulate the distribution of the drug. As stated by Norm Stamper, a spokesperson for Law Enforcement Against Prohibition, "There's a simple but profound stroke that can drive the cartels and the street traffickers out of business—end the prohibition model and replace it with a regulatory model."[27] As a bonus the government could tax the drug, just as it does alcohol and tobacco, generating revenues to offset any social costs that result from the use of the drug, such as addiction treatment programs.

Opponents reject the notion that legalization of marijuana would eliminate the black market for the drug and its attendant crime. More likely, they maintain, a black market would continue to exist as dealers attempt to evade government regulations and taxes and undercut the legitimate market. As columnist Patt Morrison states, "Legalization . . . wouldn't do away with pot-related crime entirely. There would still be a black market, just as there is in other regulated substances, such as cigarettes and liquor. That means police and prosecution, which cost money."[28]

In the end, marijuana legalization opponents insist, the increased tax revenue from the regulated sale of marijuana would not provide a huge windfall or compensate for the harms that legalization of the drug would produce. As the editors of the *Christian Science Monitor* state:

A Michigan caregiver displays the state-issued cards that allow him to legally grow enough marijuana to supply three patients. Under Michigan law, he can grow up to 12 plants per patient.

No one has figured out what the exact social costs of legalizing marijuana would be. But ephemeral taxes won't cover them—nor should society want to encourage easier access to a drug that can lead to dependency, has health risks, and reduces alertness, to name just a few of its negative outcomes. Why legalize a third substance that produces ill effects, when the US has such a poor record in dealing with the two big "licits"—alcohol and tobacco?[29]

Legalization for Medical Use

In addition to efforts to decriminalize and legalize marijuana for recreational use, advocates seek to legalize the drug as medicine. To date, marijuana has been legalized for medical purposes in 14 states. In each of these states, patients are allowed to possess and use marijuana if recommended by a doctor. Most of the 14 states also allow patients to grow small amounts of marijuana. In addition, patients may be assisted by a caregiver, who may legally help the patient grow, acquire, or use marijuana. The quantity of marijuana that patients can legally possess varies among states and generally ranges from 1 to 24 ounces (28.35 to 640 g) of marijuana and 2 to 24 plants.

In order to qualify for protection under the law in most states, patients must possess documentation that they have been diagnosed with a specific illness stated in the law. California is the exception to this rule; its law allows doctors wide discretion in deciding which patients would benefit from marijuana. Because marijuana remains a Schedule I drug under federal law, doctors cannot write prescriptions for it. Moreover, since marijuana is not available in pharmacies, prescriptions would be useless. Therefore, rather than a prescription, in most of the 14 states, doctors simply write a letter stating that they recommend marijuana for the patient. In some states medical records will suffice. Some states maintain a registry, or list, of medical marijuana patients and issue medical marijuana ID cards. In most of the 14 states with medical marijuana laws, possession of marijuana by qualified patients is allowed, even if the drug was obtained illegally.

These state laws have come in direct conflict with federal law, under which the drug remains illegal for medical as well as nonmedical uses. In 2005 the U.S. Supreme Court ruled in *Gonzalez v. Raich* that the federal government may enforce federal marijuana laws even in states that have legalized medical marijuana. Simply put, medical marijuana users in states with medical marijuana laws are safe from prosecution under state law but are vulnerable to prosecution under federal law. However, 99 percent of marijuana enforcement is conducted by state and local authorities, not federal authorities. Moreover, federal authorities typically target large-scale growing and distribution operations, not individual users. And in October 2009 the U.S. Department of Justice issued a memo directing federal attorneys not to prosecute medical marijuana users and suppliers who are in compliance with state laws. Therefore, legitimate medical marijuana users in the 14 states with medical marijuana laws enjoy a great deal of legal protection.

Regulating Medical Marijuana Suppliers

In responding to the spreading legalization of medical marijuana in the states, the federal government has primarily targeted suppliers rather than patients or caregivers. Only two states—New Mexico and Rhode Island—provide for state-run systems for the distribution of medical marijuana, and these systems are in their infancy. In most of the remaining states, patients must grow their own marijuana or obtain it from dealers operating outside the law (or at least in a gray area of the law). In a few states—mainly California and Colorado—dispensaries that are unregulated by the state have sprung up to distribute marijuana to medical patients. Colorado has about 60 dispensaries; however, California has several hundred, perhaps more than 1,000. The legality of California's dispensaries—even under state law—is debated. As a result, the federal government has raided and shut down many dispensaries, arresting their operators and seizing their inventories.

The legal climate for medical marijuana dispensaries could change as a result of the October 2009 Justice Department memo on medical marijuana. In addition to directing U.S. attorneys not to prosecute medical marijuana users, it instructs officials not to target medical marijuana providers that are in compliance with state laws. The impact of this policy shift remains to be seen. One potential problem is the lack of clarity regarding the types of distribution systems allowed under state laws. In addition, the Justice Department memo explicitly states that marijuana remains illegal under federal law and that the government is still committed to prosecuting illegal marijuana traffickers. Moreover, the memo gives U.S. attorneys discretion to prosecute medical marijuana suppliers who violate state laws, operate for profit, sell to minors, traffic in other drugs, or engage in other criminal activities. The memo states: "Prosecution of commercial enterprises that unlawfully market and sell marijuana for profit continues to be an enforcement priority of the Department."[30]

To confuse the issue even further, many counties and cities have also struggled with how to regulate dispensaries. In Colorado and Washington, as well as in California, local leaders have established

> "There's a simple but profound stroke that can drive the cartels and the street traffickers out of business—end the prohibition model and replace it with a regulatory model."[27]
>
> — Norm Stamper, former chief of police for Seattle, Washington, and spokesperson for Law Enforcement Against Prohibition, an organization that advocates drug legalization.

A Los Angeles dispensary displays several varieties of medical marijuana. In 2009, the U.S. Department of Justice instructed federal authorities to not prosecute users and providers of medical marijuana who are in compliance with state laws legalizing its use.

guidelines to limit the number of dispensaries and prevent their operation near schools. Some jurisdictions have banned dispensaries or imposed moratoriums on new outlets. In some cases the courts have gotten involved in the legality of moratoriums. Thus, due to the complicated mix of federal, state, and local laws, the future of medical marijuana dispensaries remains unclear.

Medical Marijuana Policy Aims

Advocates of medical marijuana seek to expand the legality of the drug for medical purposes in several ways. At the state level, they are currently working to add Arizona and several other states to the 14 that already have medical marijuana laws. In addition, they are working to change the classification of marijuana under the Controlled Substances Act from a Schedule I to a Schedule II drug like morphine or cocaine, which would allow doctors to prescribe it, or even a Schedule III drug, a class of substances with an even lower potential for abuse or dependence. Proponents of medical marijuana also oppose the federal government's actions in raiding dispensaries, especially since patients sometimes get swept up in such enforcement operations.

On the other hand, critics of medical marijuana oppose the further legalization of the drug for medical uses. Perhaps the strongest opponent of medical marijuana is the federal government. Various federal agencies concerned with drug policy contend the medical benefits of the drug—particularly in its smoked form—have not been proved. The White House Office of National Drug Control Policy (ONDCP) states, "Simply put, the smoked form of marijuana is not considered modern medicine."[31] Similarly, the U.S. Food and Drug Administration (FDA) rejects the idea that smoked marijuana is safe and effective. The agency states that extensive research into the issue "concluded that no sound scientific studies supported medical use of marijuana for treatment in the United States, and no animal or human data supported the safety or efficacy of marijuana for general medical use."[32] In July 2009 Gil Kerlikowske, the director of the ONDCP, stated, "Marijuana is dangerous and has no medical benefit."[33]

In addition to rejecting the safety and usefulness of smoked medical marijuana, opponents argue that the legalization of cannabis for medical purposes is a Trojan horse—a dishonest first step toward the legalization of the drug for nonmedical use. John Cooke, a sheriff in Colorado, holds this view. "The proponents of medical marijuana disingenuously use the tragic stories of truly ill people to advance the proponents' real motive of legalizing marijuana,"[34] he says. Critics contend that many of the "patients" obtaining medical marijuana in states that have legalized the drug are not truly sick but are instead abusing the system in order to gain access to the drug for recreational use.

"Marijuana is dangerous and has no medical benefit." [33]

— Gil Kerlikowske, director of the White House Office of National Drug Control Policy.

An Uncertain Future

America's marijuana policy is in flux. Thirteen states have decriminalized the drug, and many cities have made enforcing marijuana laws a low priority. In addition, 14 states have legalized marijuana for medical purposes. Witnessing this trend, many observers perceive a slow wave of legalization spreading across the nation. At the same time, more and more countries are relaxing their marijuana laws. Will the United States adopt a nationwide policy of decriminalization? Will the drug be legalized and sold at the local market along with cigarettes and beer? Most experts predict that, rather than a national policy of decriminalization or legalization, the country is likely to see a continuation of the pattern of incremental change at the state and local levels that has occurred over the past several decades.

Facts

- A 2009 Rasmussen poll found that 52 percent of Democrats favor legalizing and taxing marijuana, while only 28 percent of Republicans support this policy.

- According to a July 2009 CBS News poll, 44 percent of men support the legalization of marijuana, while 39 percent of women support legalization.

- In Britain marijuana is defined as a "Class B" drug, which means it is a controlled substance and that possession of the drug is punishable by up to five years in prison.

- In 2009 Argentina's Supreme Court ruled that it was unconstitutional to arrest people for possession of a small amount of marijuana, thus opening the door to drug law reforms in that country.

- In addition to parts of the United States, a few other countries have legalized marijuana as medicine, including Canada, Chile, and Spain.

CHAPTER THREE

How Would Legalization Affect Society?

Much of the debate over the legalization of marijuana for recreational use centers on what impacts legalizing the drug would have on society. Some contend that marijuana is a harmful substance whose use should be discouraged. Legalizing the drug could send the signal that it is safe, make it more readily obtainable, and entice more people to try it. Others argue that the harms of marijuana have been exaggerated and that legalizing the drug would not lead to a dramatic spike in use. Moreover, legalization could actually help society by reducing the crime and violence associated with the illegal drug trade. In short, both sides in the debate want to improve public health, safety, and well-being, but each side has a drastically different vision for how to achieve that goal.

How Harmful Is Marijuana?

Central to the debate over the legalization of marijuana is the disagreement over how harmful the drug is to human health. While there are some points of disagreement on this issue, some facts are well-established. For example, marijuana is known to have short-term effects on a person's perceptions and memory. One study published in the *Journal of the American Medical Association* found that heavy marijuana users had an impaired ability to pay attention, remember, and learn 24 hours after their last use of the drug. Another study found that frequent marijuana users had problems with math skills, verbal expression, and memory recall. These

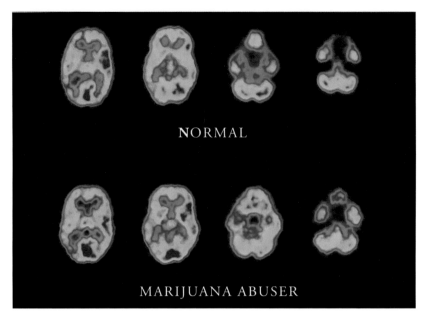

NORMAL

MARIJUANA ABUSER

The effects of THC, the psychoactive drug found in marijuana, can be seen in colored scans comparing the brain of a marijuana user (bottom) with the brain of a non-user (top). The front of the brain is uppermost in these scans, which show progressively deeper slices from left to right. The cerebellum, which controls coordination and spatial judgment, can be seen in the lower parts of the four scans that are farthest right. The color red denotes brain activity. Red areas of high activity can be seen in the cerebellum of the non-user. This activity is largely absent from the cerebellum of the marijuana user, which would result in lack of coordination and poor spatial judgment.

effects are especially harmful to young people. As stated by the White House Office of National Drug Control Policy (ONDCP), the agency of the federal government that oversees the nation's drug control strategy, "Effects such as these may be especially problematic during teens' peak learning years, when their brains are still developing."[35]

Researchers have studied the brains of adolescents in an attempt to understand the harms of marijuana. In a 2009 study published in the *Journal of Psychiatric Research*, doctors scanned the brains of young men who reported that they had smoked marijuana between the ages of 13 and 19. The researchers found abnormalities in brain regions involved in memory, attention, language, decision-making, and executive-functioning skills, which include the ability to control, monitor, and plan one's behaviors. Those findings suggest that marijuana may cause permanent impairment in all of these areas of functioning.

In addition, marijuana also affects a user's perception of time and space and the ability to react quickly to changing circumstances. Therefore, people who drive while under the influence of marijuana have an increased risk of accidents. The National Highway Traffic Safety Administration conducted a study that measured drivers' reaction times as well as how frequently they checked the rearview mirror, side streets, and the relative speed of other vehicles. The study concluded that even a moderate dose of marijuana-impaired driving performance, thus placing the driver and others at risk of potentially fatal accidents.

Because marijuana is inhaled, experts say it carries some health risks that are similar to the risks of cigarettes. Mark Porter, a physician and medical correspondent for the *Times*, a London, England, newspaper, writes: "Most people consider cannabis to be much safer than tobacco but, drag for drag, it is actually more harmful. Cannabis smoke is far more acrid than tobacco and causes more damage to the lining of the airways. . . . And, like tobacco, it is packed with carcinogens."[36] Studies have shown that heavy marijuana users experience many of the same respiratory problems as tobacco smokers, including an increased risk of lung infections. However, while cannabis contains carcinogens, studies have failed to prove that smoking it causes cancer of the lung, upper respiratory tract, or upper digestive tract. As stated by the National Institute on Drug Abuse (NIDA), the department of the federal government that oversees all marijuana research in the United States, "The link between marijuana smoking and these cancers remains unsubstantiated at this time."[37]

Mental Illness

Beyond the physical harms of marijuana, researchers have also concluded that the drug may cause or at least contribute to psychiatric disorders. Numerous studies have shown a correlation between heavy marijuana use and mental illnesses such as anxiety disorders, depression, and schizophrenia. People who start smoking marijuana at a young age are especially at risk for mental illness. However, researchers are not sure what this correlation means. They have three possible explanations: (1) marijuana causes mental illnesses, (2) marijuana makes mental illnesses worse, or (3) people with preexisting mental illnesses use marijuana to make themselves feel better.

Researchers have become especially alarmed over the potential for marijuana to cause psychotic symptoms such as paranoia and hallucinations (hearing or seeing things that other people do not hear or see). As NIDA states, "High doses of marijuana

"High doses of marijuana can produce an acute psychotic reaction."[38]

— National Institute on Drug Abuse, an agency of the federal government that oversees research on the causes and treatments of drug abuse.

can produce an acute psychotic reaction." Moreover, according to NIDA, "use of the drug may trigger the onset or relapse of schizophrenia in vulnerable individuals."[38] Schizophrenia is an extremely disabling, chronic psychotic disorder that can leave a person impaired for life. Thus, the idea that marijuana may cause it or contribute to its onset is cause for concern.

Experts believe that the potential for marijuana to cause psychosis (as well as other mental problems) has grown in recent years due to a rise in the potency of the drug. Marijuana growers have used cross-breeding techniques to produce strains with increasingly higher levels of THC, the plant's high-inducing chemical. According to the federal government, the average THC level in marijuana has increased from under 4 percent in 1983 to over 10 percent in 2009;

An Environmental Threat

Many marijuana farmers grow their crops on public lands, including in national parks and forests. Their farms, known as "gardens" or "grows," are especially common in western states such as California, Oregon, and Washington but have also sprung up in Georgia and Tennessee. Many grows are run by Mexican drug cartels, who have found that it is easier to cultivate crops in the United States than to smuggle their product across the border. These operations pose a significant threat to the environment. The growers typically clear the land, divert water from streams, scatter toxic pesticides, and generate piles of trash and human waste that are left behind when they abandon the sites. John Heil, a regional press officer for the U.S. Forest Service, says, "We look at this as ecological disaster." Proponents of legalization cite grows as just one more consequence of marijuana prohibition. Legalizing marijuana, they say, would take the profit incentive out of such operations, thereby helping to conserve the environment.

Quoted in Marc Benjamin, "Illegal Marijuana Farms Scar Sierra Landscape," *Fresno (CA) Bee*, July 23, 2009. www.fresnobee.com.

some strains are as high as 30 percent. This trend is especially troubling to public health officials due to the high rate of marijuana use by young people. According to the National Survey on Drug Use and Health, of the 2.1 million Americans who used marijuana for the first time in 2007, 62 percent were under 18.

Addiction

In addition to the possible physical, mental, and psychological harms caused by marijuana, experts say addiction is also a concern. A substance is considered addictive if a regular user has withdrawal symptoms when denied access to the drug; these symptoms typically include high blood pressure, an accelerated heart rate, anxiety, and craving for the drug. While marijuana is not as physically addictive as other narcotics, such as heroin, cocaine, or methamphetamine, experts have found that some heavy users do become dependent on the drug. According to NIDA, "Long-term marijuana abusers trying to quit report irritability, sleeplessness, decreased appetite, anxiety, and drug craving."[39] The 1999 Institute of Medicine report found that 9 percent of marijuana users become dependent on the drug. In addition, according to the Substance Abuse and Mental Health Services Administration (SAMHSA), a government agency that oversees the nation's mental health and substance abuse treatment, 287,933 people sought treatment for addiction primarily to marijuana in 2007, a 4 percent increase from 1997.

Of particular concern is the number of young people receiving treatment for addiction to marijuana. According to SAMHSA, of those who received treatment for marijuana addiction in 2007, 41 percent—more than 115,000—were under 19. Experts contend that the emotional development of these marijuana-addicted teens is stymied. As stated by Annie Ramniceanu, the clinical director at Spectrum Youth and Family Services in Vermont, marijuana-dependent teens "don't deal with anything. They never learned how to have fun without smoking pot, never learned how to deal with conflict."[40]

Less Harmful than Alcohol and Tobacco

Most proponents of legalization concede that cannabis poses some risks, especially for heavy users, and that teens should not

"Overall, by comparison with other drugs used mainly for 'recreational' purposes, cannabis could be rated to be a relatively safe drug."[42]

— Leslie Iversen, a professor of pharmacology at Oxford University.

be allowed to use it. However, they insist that the drug is no more harmful—perhaps even safer—than other legal substances such as alcohol and tobacco. As stated by Rob Kampia, executive director of the Marijuana Policy Project, an organization that advocates the legalization of marijuana, "Compared with alcohol, marijuana is less addictive, much less toxic, and overwhelmingly less likely to provoke violence."[41] Leslie Iversen, a professor of pharmacology at Oxford University, agrees: "Overall, by comparison with other drugs used mainly for 'recreational' purposes, cannabis could be rated to be a relatively safe drug."[42]

Legalization proponents dispute the claim that marijuana is more harmful to the lungs than tobacco. For one thing, they point out, marijuana users inhale a smaller quantity of smoke than do cigarette smokers. The Drug Policy Alliance (DPA) Network, an organization that favors liberalizing the nation's drug laws, states: "Like tobacco smoke, marijuana smoke contains a number of irritants and carcinogens. But marijuana users typically smoke much less often than tobacco smokers, and over time, inhale much less smoke. As a result, the risk of serious lung damage should be lower in marijuana smokers."[43] The DPA Network goes on to cite the lack of evidence that marijuana causes lung cancer, a fact that NIDA acknowledges.

Exaggerated Concerns?

In addition to dismissing the physical harms of marijuana, legalization advocates are also skeptical about the claims that the drug causes mental illnesses such as schizophrenia. They emphasize the fact, conceded by researchers, that while mentally ill people appear more likely to smoke marijuana, there is no proof that marijuana is the *cause* of mental illness. As explained by Paul Armentano, the deputy director of the National Organization for the Reform of Marijuana Laws, "Confounding factors (such as poverty, family history, polydrug use, etc.) make it difficult, if not impossible, for researchers to adequately determine whether any cause-and-effect relationship exists between cannabis use and mental illness." Armentano adds that mentally ill people may actually use marijuana to help them feel better, a possibility that researchers acknowledge. He writes,

"Many experts point out that this association [between cannabis use and mental illness] may be due to patients' self-medicating with cannabis."[44] In particular, advocates of legalization contend that the relationship between cannabis and schizophrenia is complex. Some chemicals in marijuana might actually help users control psychotic symptoms, while others might make them worse.

Concerns about addiction are also exaggerated, say proponents of legalization. They contend that the risk of addiction to marijuana is slight, but certainly much less than the risk of addiction to alcohol or cigarettes. Any addiction that does result, they argue, is mild and short-term. Legalization advocates concede that any level of addiction is undesirable. However, they maintain, it is illogical to argue that marijuana should be kept illegal because it is addictive, while tobacco and alcohol—which are much more addictive—are legal.

Advocates maintain that proof of marijuana's relative harmlessness can be seen in the large number of successful people who have used the drug. Joe Conason, a columnist for *Salon*, notes that many great athletes have admitted to smoking marijuana, including Olympic swimmer Michael Phelps, professional football player Mark Stepnoski, and professional basketball player Josh Howard. They are joined by leaders of other fields, including scientists Margaret Mead and Carl Sagan, business leaders Richard Branson and Bill Gates, and musicians Duke Ellington and Bob Dylan. In addition, two recent presidents, Bill Clinton and Barack Obama, admitted to past marijuana use. In light of this list of prominent marijuana users, Conason asks, "Why should the law treat cannabis as a damaging addiction when in fact nearly anyone who has accomplished anything worthwhile seems to have taken at least a toke or two?"[45]

Would Legalization Mean More Drug Use?

In addition to debating the harms of marijuana on human health, legalization opponents and proponents disagree over whether legalizing the drug would lead to more drug use. Opponents contend that marijuana use would increase under a policy of legalization. This rise in use would result from a combination of factors, they say. First, legalization would send the message to society that marijuana is a harmless drug. Second, removal of criminal sanctions would lessen the fear and stigma associated with marijuana's use. Third, the creation of a legal market for the drug would lead to a greater supply and lower prices. All of these forces would draw people in greater numbers to marijuana, critics charge.

To study the potential impact of legalization on drug use, experts have examined patterns of drug use in countries that have loosened their marijuana laws. While no country has yet legalized marijuana, the Netherlands has come the closest with its system of de facto legalization. In 1976 the Netherlands ceased enforcement of laws against possession and sale of small amounts of marijuana in a policy known as depenalization. In the mid-1980s it gradually

The Risks of Teen Marijuana Use

Not every teen who smokes marijuana will become an addict. However, according to the National Institute on Drug Abuse, about 10 percent of people who use marijuana will become dependent on the drug. This fact is illustrated by the story of Michael, whose last name was withheld to protect his privacy. Michael smoked his first marijuana cigarette at the age of 12 because, he says, "I wanted my friends to accept me." Before long, Michael was a daily marijuana user. He explains how the drug took over his life: "I just lost focus of everything. School was boring. I used to like going to church. Smoking marijuana drew me away. I was a DJ and I stopped DJing. I couldn't even focus on that. I just wanted to get my next high, to find more money to smoke." He began stealing and selling crack cocaine to make money for his habit and was eventually arrested. After serving a sentence in a youth correctional facility, Michael, now 18, entered a drug rehabilitation center because, he says, "I wanted to be out there living my life and not using drugs."

Quoted in Karen Fanning, "Marijuana Mess," *Choices*, April/May 2009, pp. 9–11.

initiated an even more liberal policy of de facto legalization, allowing coffee shops to sell the drug to adults without fear of prosecution. There is little research into the effect of this policy on drug use. However, several studies show that marijuana use among adolescents increased dramatically after the arrival of cannabis-selling coffee shops in the mid-1980s.

One study published in *Science* magazine found that the number of Dutch youths between the age of 18 and 20 who reported using marijuana during a 30-day period more than doubled between 1984 and 1996—from 8.5 percent to 18.8 percent. During the same time period, the number of Dutch youths between 18 and 20 who reported using marijuana at least once nearly tripled—from 15 percent to 44 percent. Assessing all the research on the effect of the liberalization of marijuana laws in the Netherlands, researcher George S. Yacoubian Jr. concludes, "The evidence, though antiquated and sparse, seems to suggest that while depenalization had little effect on subsequent rates of marijuana use, de facto legalization (i.e., proliferation of coffee shops) led to sharp increases of marijuana use among Dutch youth."[46]

A coffee shop employee in the Netherlands prepares marijuana cigarettes for sale to customers. The Netherlands has one of the most liberal marijuana policies in the world. Coffee shops are allowed to sell marijuana to adults without fear of prosecution.

For comparison, during this same time period in the United States, where drug policies remained stringent, the rates of adolescent marijuana use declined. According to the Monitoring the Future Study, an annual survey of American students, the rate of 30-day marijuana use by high school seniors decreased from 25.2 percent in 1986 to 21.9 percent in 1996. The lifetime rate of marijuana use by high school seniors decreased from 54.9 percent in 1984 to 44.9 percent in 1996. Thus, while the rate of use increased in the Netherlands under de facto legalization, it decreased in the United States under prohibition. However, despite legalization in the Netherlands, marijuana use among youths there remained slightly lower than among youths in the United States. This fact suggests that there may be cultural differences between the 2 countries that lead to more marijuana use in the United States.

In fact, despite the rise of marijuana use among Dutch youths following de facto legalization, some studies have found that, taking all age groups into account, the overall rate of marijuana use in the Netherlands today remains much lower than in the United States. For example, a 2008 study conducted by the World Health Organization found that the percentage of the population that has used marijuana in the Netherlands is less than half that of the United States, at 19.8 percent and 42.4 percent, respectively. Americans also start using marijuana at a much younger age. The percentage of youths who have tried marijuana by age 15 in the Netherlands is 7 percent, compared to 20.2 percent in the United States. Based on these and other findings, the authors of this report concluded that "drug use . . . does not appear to be simply related to drug policy, since countries with more stringent policies towards illegal drug use did not have lower levels of such drug use than countries with more liberal policies."[47]

Fuel for Both Sides

Both sides of the marijuana legalization debate cite the case of the Netherlands to support their position. Opponents of legalization point to the rise in adolescent marijuana use that occurred after de facto legalization in the Netherlands and argue that the same thing would happen in the United States under legalization. Proponents of legalization cite the fact that despite de facto legalization, the rate of marijuana use overall is much lower in the Netherlands than in the United States. Thus, legalizing marijuana in the United States would not lead to a massive surge of new marijuana users.

Some legalization advocates concede that making the drug legal could result in a rise in use, at least initially. However, they downplay the extent or seriousness of this increase. Some contend the increase in use would be temporary and would quickly reverse once the new smokers had satisfied their curiosity. Others suggest that the rise in use might in part be a result of people switching to marijuana from alcohol and tobacco, which are arguably more dangerous drugs, thus resulting in an overall benefit to society. "After all," states blogger and columnist Kevin Drum, "excessive drinking causes nearly 80,000 deaths per year in the United States, compared to virtually none for pot. Trading alcohol consumption for cannabis use might be a pretty attractive deal."[48]

> "Legalizing marijuana is unlikely to quiet Mexico's drug war."[50]
>
> — *Christian Science Monitor*, a national newspaper.

Legalization's Effects on Crime and Violence

In addition to disagreement over the risks posed by marijuana and the potential increase in marijuana use, there is also debate over how legalizing marijuana would affect the crime and violence associated with the drug trade. Because marijuana is currently illegal for recreational use, it can only be bought and sold on the black market. This situation creates inflated prices and allows violent gangs to reap huge profits by smuggling the drug into the United States. According to the U.S. Department of Justice, Mexican drug cartels make more money from distributing marijuana in the United States than from any other source. In recent years these gangs have murdered over 7,000 people—mostly rival gang members and Mexican police—in their attempts to corner the drug market.

Advocates argue that legalizing the drug would end the demand for illegal marijuana and thereby eliminate the violent marijuana trade. As explained by Arizona attorney general Terry Goddard, "The violence that we see in Mexico is fueled 65 percent to 70 percent by the trade in one drug: marijuana. I've called for at least a rational discussion as to what our country can do to take the profit out of that."[49]

Is Marijuana a Gateway Drug?

Opponents of legalizing marijuana contend that marijuana is a gateway drug—that is, smoking marijuana opens the door to the use of other, even more harmful substances such as cocaine and heroin. In fact, studies have shown that most people who use other illegal drugs use marijuana first. According to the U.S. Drug Enforcement Administration, "Using marijuana sometimes lowers inhibitions about drug use and exposes users to a culture that encourages use of other drugs."

Advocates of legalization reject the gateway theory. They acknowledge that most people who use hard drugs have also used marijuana, but they argue that this is not the same as saying that marijuana leads to other types of drug use. In fact, they contend that most marijuana users *do not* use hard drugs, thus disproving the gateway theory. As stated by the Drug Policy Alliance Network, an organization that favors legalization, "For the large majority of people, marijuana is a terminus rather than a gateway drug."

U.S. Drug Enforcement Administration, "Exposing the Myth of Smoked Medical Marijuana." http://justice.gov.

Drug Policy Alliance Network, "Myths and Facts About Marijuana." www.drugpolicy.org.

Opponents of legalization reject the idea that legalizing marijuana would end the violence perpetrated by Mexican drug cartels. They contend that although marijuana makes up the largest share of the volume of illegal drugs trafficked in the United States, it is not the most profitable drug and therefore does not provoke the most violence. As the editors of the *Christian Science Monitor* explain: "It's the dollars that count, and the big earners—cocaine, methamphetamine, heroin—play a much larger role in crime and violence. In recent years, Mexico has become a major cocaine route to the US. That's what's fanning the violence . . ., so legalizing marijuana is unlikely to quiet Mexico's drug war."[50]

An Enduring Debate

The impact that the legalization of marijuana would have on society is unknown. Opponents insist that it would lead to an increase in marijuana use, especially among young people. This rise in cannabis use would in turn harm the physical and mental health of Americans. Proponents, on the other hand, insist that any increase in marijuana use would be small, the harms limited, and the costs offset by the benefits to society of reduced drug-related violence. This debate is likely to continue as long as marijuana plants sprout and spread their distinctive five-pointed leaves.

Facts

- According to the U.S. Drug Enforcement Administration, marijuana contains over 400 chemicals, including most of the harmful chemicals found in tobacco smoke.

- According to the Substance Abuse and Mental Health Services Administration, marijuana was involved in 290,563 hospital emergency department visits in 2006, the last year for which statistics are available.

- A poll conducted by Rasmussen in 2009 found that 46 percent of Americans believe marijuana is a gateway drug that leads to use of harder drugs, while 37 percent reject this theory.

- Many famous people have been arrested for marijuana possession, including filmmaker Oliver Stone, singer Whitney Houston, rapper Snoop Doggy Dog, guitarist Carlos Santana, basketball star Allen Iverson, and author Ken Kesey.

- The Monitoring the Future survey reports that 52 percent of twelfth-grade students see "great risk" in using marijuana regularly. That number is 65 percent among tenth graders and 72 percent among eighth graders.

CHAPTER FOUR

How Would Legalization Affect the Economy?

I n the spring of 2009, California was in a budget crisis, facing the prospect of slashing social services, laying off workers, closing schools, and sending IOUs in lieu of payments to vendors. Confronted with these dire circumstances, some advocated legalizing and taxing marijuana as a means of generating state revenue. In fact, a majority of residents appeared open to this solution; one poll found that 56 percent of California voters favored such a policy. When presented with this statistic at a press conference, California governor Arnold Schwarzenegger said he was not currently in favor of marijuana legalization. However, he went on to say, "I think it's time for a debate. . . . I think we ought to study very carefully what other countries are doing that have legalized marijuana and other drugs, what effect did it have on those countries?"[51]

Some commentators believe Schwarzenegger's openness to the idea of marijuana legalization reflects a growing public acceptance of the idea as a solution to the struggling economy—not only at the state level, but at the national level as well. In addition to the poll showing that 56 percent of Californians supported legalization, a Zogby poll found that 52 percent of Americans nationwide favored the policy as a means of shoring up the national economy. As stated by Ethan Nadelmann, the executive director of the Drug

Policy Alliance Network, an organization that favors alternatives to drug prohibition, "The discussion about regulating and taxing marijuana now has an air of legitimacy to it that it didn't quite have before. And the economy has given the issue a real turbo-charge."[52]

Potential Economic Benefits

Those who favor the legalization of marijuana make several economic arguments to support their position. First, they contend that legalization would allow the government to tax the drug, thus generating much-needed revenue to offset budget deficits.

In addition to bringing in cash, supporters maintain, legalizing marijuana would cut government costs associated with enforcing marijuana laws. Each year, the federal, state, and local governments spend $44 billion fighting the war on drugs. This money is spent on efforts to interdict drugs being smuggled into the country, to root out major dealers and suppliers, and to fight the violent crime connected with the black market for drugs. Legalization supporters say that removing marijuana from the list of illicit substances would save the government billions of dollars. They point out that more than 800,000 Americans are arrested each year on marijuana charges, creating expenditures for police, courts, and prisons. Legalizing marijuana would essentially eliminate all these costs.

Some advocates point out that even decriminalization, a less drastic step than legalization, can reap economic benefits. Making possession and use of small amounts of the drug a civil violation rather than a criminal offense eliminates the cost of arrest and incarceration for what many consider to be nonviolent, low-level infractions of the law. In addition, in most jurisdictions where marijuana has been decriminalized, violators must pay a fine if caught in possession of the drug, thus generating government revenue. In July 2009 Cook County, Illinois, passed a law that imposes a $200 fine on first-time marijuana offenders, joining several other counties in the state with similar ordinances. In Sangamon County, for example, the government collected $46,000 in fines for marijuana possession in 2008.

"It would be an enormous economic stimulus if we stopped wasting so much money arresting and locking people up for nonviolent drug offenses and instead brought new tax revenue from legal sales."[53]

— Jack Cole, executive director of Law Enforcement Against Prohibition, an organization that promotes the legalization of marijuana and other drugs.

Calculating Savings and Income

Economists have attempted to quantify the economic benefits of marijuana legalization. After studying the issue, Jeffrey A. Miron, an economics professor at Harvard University, estimates that the federal government spends $2.9 billion per year arresting, prosecuting, and incarcerating marijuana offenders. State and local governments spend an estimated $10 billion on these enforcement costs. Thus, he concludes, legalizing marijuana would save the government $12.9 billion per year. In addition, he concludes, if marijuana were taxed at a rate similar to tobacco and alcohol, the government would receive $6.7 billion in taxes annually from legalization of the drug. Therefore, according to Miron's research, the overall benefit of marijuana legalization to governments would be $19.6 billion.

Another study found an even greater economic benefit from marijuana legalization. Jon Gettman, a marijuana legalization activist who received a PhD in public policy from George Mason University, reviewed government statistics on the issue. He concludes that the cost of arresting marijuana users is $10.7 billion per year, a number lower than Miron's. However, he also contends that if the drug were legalized, the government would bring in $31.1 billion in taxes. Thus, according to Gettman, the overall economic benefit of marijuana legalization would be $41.8 billion—more than double Miron's figure.

The different conclusions reached by Miron and Gettman reflect different assumptions each scholar makes about the amount of marijuana that would be sold, the price of the drug, the rate at which it would be taxed, and other variables. Despite the dramatic differences, both studies give support to those who believe the legalization of marijuana could benefit the country financially.

In sum, advocates insist that the legalization of marijuana would be a boon to society. The resulting combination of fresh tax revenue and reduced enforcement costs would result in billions more dollars being available for governments to spend on needed services such as health care, education, and social programs. As stated by Jack Cole, the executive director of Law Enforcement Against Prohibition, "It would be an enormous economic stimulus if we stopped wasting so much money arresting and locking people up for nonviolent drug offenses and instead brought new tax revenue from legal sales."[53]

Law enforcement officers monitor a marijuana eradication operation in Southern California's Angeles National Forest in 2009. The government spends huge sums on such efforts but programs like this one also remove billions of dollars worth of marijuana from circulation.

The False Promise of Economic Benefits

Opponents argue that legalizing cannabis would do little to help the economy. First, they contend that legalizing the drug would not necessarily result in huge tax revenues. Mark Kleiman, a professor of public policy at the University of California at Los Angeles, estimates that the illegal marijuana market generates $10 billion in revenue per year, which is only 0.1 percent of the gross domestic product (the value of the nation's total goods and services). Moreover, if the drug were legalized, the price would drop, resulting in less revenue to tax. Thus, taxing the drug would not bring in enough money to help the government significantly, Kleiman concludes. In any event, many dealers would likely opt to continue operating in a black market in order to avoid the taxes. As evidence, legalization opponents cite the example of Canada, where due to heavy taxes 30 percent of tobacco is bought on the black market tax free.

The Economy of the Emerald Triangle

Much of California's lucrative—and mostly illegal—marijuana crop is grown in the three northern California counties of Humboldt, Mendocino, and Trinity, an area known as the Emerald Triangle (emerald for the green color of the marijuana plants that thrive there). Due to the region's rainy climate, the marijuana grown there is high-quality and extremely valuable. The growth and sale of the drug infuses large sums of money into the local economies. According to one report, marijuana raises the retail buying power of Mendocino County residents by $58 million per year. However, some residents fear that legalization of marijuana could have a negative impact on local growers and the businesses that depend on them. Under legalization, the price of the drug would decline, reducing the value of the harvest. According to Mendocino County resident Keith Campbell: "It would hurt the economy here because the price would drop. Once it's legal, the growers out in the back woods can't get those [high] prices anymore. And everyone down here in town feels it."

Quoted in Robert Price, "Taxing Quandary: Legalize Marijuana to Increase State Revenue and Scale Back Violence, or Maintain America's Difficult War on Drugs?" *Bakersfield Californian*, July 26, 2009. www.bakersfield.com.

Critics also take issue with the claim that legalization of marijuana would save government money in police, court, and imprisonment costs. Legalization opponents reject the common argument that the jails and prisons are full of nonviolent offenders whose only crime was to smoke marijuana. They contend that many people arrested for marijuana are caught up in other crimes as well and would end up in jail or prison regardless of the legal status of marijuana. As the White House Office of National Drug Control Policy states, "One of the primary arguments used by drug legalization advocates is based on a lie—that our prisons are filled with marijuana smokers. In fact, the vast majority of drug prisoners are violent criminals, repeat offenders, traffickers, or all of the above."[54] The ONDCP reports that only 1.4 percent of state prisoners are being held on charges related only to marijuana, and only 0.3 percent are being held for marijuana possession (as opposed to sales or trafficking) as their only charge. Thus, eliminating the cost of incarcerating marijuana arrestees will save the government little money.

In addition to failing to cut prison costs, according to opponents, legalization would do little to lessen the cost of the war on drugs. The bulk of the money spent on the prevention of drug trafficking and dealing is dedicated to stopping the flow of heroin, cocaine, and methamphetamine, critics explain. According to Kevin A. Sabet, a former official at the ONDCP, "Marijuana's share of the black market is modest (the cocaine market is three times larger)."[55] Because the marijuana market does not produce the levels of crime and violence associated with other drugs, critics say that legalization would do little to cut law-enforcement costs connected to the illegal drug trade.

Too Many Costs

Opponents believe that legalization would actually cost more money than it saves. The expense of setting up a system to regulate and tax the drug could be significant. As stated by Rosalie Pacula, a scholar at the Rand Corporation, a public policy research organization, "I have a hard time believing the tax revenue would offset the full cost of regulating the drug."[56]

In addition to the cost of regulation, critics maintain, legalization would saddle the government with social costs. They contend that legalizing marijuana would remove the stigma and fear surrounding the drug. This official sanctioning of marijuana, combined with its new low price, would lead to an increase in its use. Estimates of this increase in use range from 30 percent to 60 percent; some experts predict that use of the drug could double. This increase in turn would lead to a host of social ills that would require government money to address. As stated by Sabet, "Accidents would

"One of the primary arguments used by drug legalization advocates is based on a lie—that our prisons are filled with marijuana smokers. In fact, the vast majority of drug prisoners are violent criminals, repeat offenders, traffickers, or all of the above."[54]

— White House Office of National Drug Control Policy, the agency of the federal government responsible for formulating the nation's drug control strategy.

increase, healthcare costs would rise and productivity would suffer." He cites the example of alcohol to illustrate the costs that legalized marijuana would impose. "The $8 billion in tax revenue generated from [alcohol] does little to offset the nearly $200 billion in social costs attributed to its use."[57]

One of the major costs that society will be forced to bear, according to legalization opponents, is the price of treating a new group of people who have become addicted to marijuana and other drugs. As stated by Lori Green, a spokesperson and parental advocate for the Coalition for a Drug Free California, the argument that legalizing marijuana will help the economy is "just another tactic to mainstream marijuana use into our everyday life. Later on, we're going to pay triple or more in costs of new addictions than any new taxes are going to cover."[58] In sum, due to the increased social costs it would produce, compared with the meager tax revenue it would generate, opponents conclude that legalizing marijuana would do little to help the economy.

Talk of Legalizing and Taxing Marijuana in California

This debate over the economic benefits of legalizing marijuana has come to a head in California. On many issues California is a sort of social laboratory in which citizens experiment with policies that are then adopted or rejected nationally—marijuana has proved to be one such issue. In California, marijuana for recreational use was decriminalized in the 1970s; medical marijuana has been legal for more than a decade; and public support for nonmedical legalization is rising. The push to legalize and tax marijuana in California is active on several fronts: in the state capitol, in the form of government legislation; at the grassroots level, in the form of several voter initiatives; and in various city governments, in the form of efforts to tax medical marijuana.

In February 2009, California state legislator Tom Ammiano introduced a bill to legalize and tax marijuana. The Marijuana Control, Regulation, and Education Act would legalize the drug for those over 21 and subject it to sales taxes as well as a $50 per-ounce levy. Ammiano has promoted his legislation primarily as a remedy for the state's economic woes. He cites the common statistic that marijuana is California's most lucrative crop, generating $14 billion in revenue per year. That number is significantly higher than the next most profitable crops, fruits and nuts, which bring in $10.4 billion, and vegetables and melons, which bring in $8 billion. When proposing his legislation, Ammiano stated: "With the state in the midst of an historic economic crisis, the move towards regulating and taxing marijuana is simply common sense. This legislation would generate much needed revenue for the state."[59] Indeed, the California State Board of Equalization, the agency responsible for collecting taxes in the state, has concluded that the bill could generate $1.4 billion annually in revenue from taxes.

In addition to generating tax revenue, supporters argue, the law would cut costs associated with the arrest, prosecution, and incarceration of marijuana users. According to Bruce Mirken, director of communications for the Marijuana Policy Project, an organization that advocates the legalization of marijuana, the legislation "would save millions of dollars in law enforcement costs generated by California's more than 70,000 marijuana arrests each year. That's money that could be used to lock up violent criminals, or to restore school or health funding that was cut [from the] state budget."[60]

However, the tax board's research is based on various assumptions that could affect the outcome. First, the board assumes that Californians consume 1 million ounces (28.3 million g) of marijuana per year. Next, the researchers posit that if the drug were legalized, the price of marijuana would decrease 50 percent, causing consumption to increase 40 percent. However, the board predicts that the imposition of a $50-per-ounce levy would lead to another 11 percent decrease in use. Finally, the researchers note that if marijuana were legalized, some people might switch to marijuana from alcohol and tobacco, leading to a decrease in

> *"With [California] in the midst of an historic economic crisis, the move towards regulating and taxing marijuana is simply common sense."[59]*
>
> — Tom Ammiano, a Democratic state legislator in California.

Marijuana plants thrive in steep, scrub-covered canyons near Los Angeles (pictured) and in other parts of California. Experts often describe marijuana as California's most lucrative crop.

taxes from those products and negating the gains of the marijuana taxes. Due to the uncertainties around these and other factors, some question the board's findings. Kleiman, for example, believes the maximum potential revenue would be about $425 million per year, which would do little to repair a $40 billion budget gap.

Grassroots Legalization Efforts

In addition to Ammiano's legislative proposal, California has also seen a major movement to bring a marijuana legalization ballot initiative to the voters. As of September 2009, 3 groups were attempting to secure the signatures required to get their initiatives on the ballot. All 3 of these initiatives would repeal marijuana laws and require the government to regulate and tax cannabis transactions as a way to produce revenue for the state. The sponsors of the most sweeping initiative, the California Cannabis Initiative 2010, contend that among other benefits, the law would "generate an estimated $1.4 billion in revenues for California each year through taxes and fees . . . and save California millions of dollars in costs related to the criminal justice system."[61] Similarly, the group behind another initiative, Tax and Regulate Cannabis California 2010, states that its law will "tax cannabis in order to generate billions of dollars for our state and local governments to fund what matters most: jobs, healthcare, schools and libraries, parks, roads, transportation, and more."[62]

The push to use marijuana to save California's economy is not only taking place at the state level. Besides state legislation and voter initiatives, California is also seeing marijuana policy reforms at the level of local government. These policies are aimed at taxing medical marijuana. Although medical marijuana is illegal under federal law, the federal government announced in March 2009 that it would not crack down on the sale of medical marijuana in states that have approved it, including California, which now has a thriving medical marijuana industry. This development has led city leaders to consider new or increased taxes on the drug as a means of revenue.

In July 2009 the citizens of Oakland voted overwhelmingly in favor of Measure F, a city ordinance that raised the taxes paid by medical marijuana dispensaries, the stores that sell the drug to patients. The tax was raised from $1.20 per $1,000 in sales to $18 per $1,000. Oakland's city auditor estimated that the bumped-up tax could bring in $300,000 annually. However, city council member Rebecca Kaplan believes the number is much higher—perhaps $1 million—due to the rapid growth of the medical marijuana business under the lax enforcement policies of the Obama administration. She sees the public's approval of the tax as a sign of growing public acceptance of marijuana and its economic potential: "I do definitely see this as a shift in the political winds in terms of how people are talking about medical marijuana, marijuana reform and budgeting."[63]

"A billion dollars in tax revenue won't make much of a dent in California's budget. And it's small potatoes compared with what's at stake as the nation tries to come to grips with its boundless appetite for getting high and the incredible costs of that appetite."[66]

— Editors of the *Merced Sun-Star*, a California newspaper.

Potential Savings in Massachusetts

In 2008 Massachusetts voters approved Question 2, making their state the thirteenth in the nation to decriminalize marijuana. Under the new law, possession of a small amount of the drug is a civil infraction punishable by a $100 fine, rather than a misdemeanor or felony offense, which would typically result in arrest and possibly jail time. Prior to the election, Harvard University economics professor Jeffrey A. Miron conducted a study designed to measure the economic impact of the law. He estimated the savings that would result from ending the arrest, prosecution, and incarceration of marijuana offenders. In addition, he noted that decriminalization could also result in revenues from fines levied against marijuana users. However, due to uncertainty regarding how many people would be fined and how many would actually pay, he did not factor these payments into his calculation. Based on his estimations, he concluded that decriminalization could save the state $29.5 million per year in government spending.

For their part the owners of the medical marijuana dispensaries support the tax, viewing it as a way to shore up support for their business. In fact, they are the ones who approached the city council with the idea. Keith Stephenson, the executive director of a dispensary called Purple Heart Patient Center, states, "We wanted to further legitimize the medical marijuana paradigm to show that we are truly willing to assist [Oakland], and to show other cities that there are social benefits to this."[64]

In addition to Oakland, other California cities, including Los Angeles and Sacramento, are considering taxing marijuana dispensaries. In Los Angeles, council member Janice Hahn believes the government could raise $32 million a year by taxing the city's 400 medical marijuana dispensaries. She contends that this income could offset some of the cuts that have been made as the state government has tightened its belt. As she explains:

> [The state is] coming after even more money from the municipalities. It really was a motivation to say, "Hey, here's a new business. . . . Let's see how we can create a new category for cannabis and tax them on their gross sales." Maybe that will mean some services we won't have to cut, some jobs we won't have to get rid of and some police officers we can keep.[65]

The Road to Fiscal Solvency?

Not everyone agrees that legalizing and taxing marijuana is the way for California to cure its ailing economy. Many oppose the rush to reap tax dollars as a hasty and ill-conceived quick fix that could backfire in the form of increased use of marijuana and other drugs, especially by young people. Some argue that the money to be gained by taxing marijuana will do little to improve the economy or to compensate for the harms of marijuana addiction. As the editors of the *Merced Sun-Star*, a California newspaper, put it: "A billion dollars in tax revenue won't make much of a dent in California's budget. And it's small potatoes compared with what's at stake as the nation tries to come to grips with its boundless appetite for getting high and the incredible costs of that appetite."[66]

The debate in California reveals that the perceived economic benefit has become one of the primary arguments in favor of the legalization of marijuana—in California and nationwide. It remains to be seen whether the state's politicians will vote in favor of state legislation, whether its citizens will vote for a statewide initiative, or whether the taxation of medical marijuana will spread beyond Oakland, Los Angeles, and Sacramento. Moreover, it is too soon to know if other states will follow California's lead or if the nation as a whole will embrace marijuana legalization as a means to achieve fiscal solvency. However, the debate over marijuana legalization is sure to continue as policy makers around the country look for creative ways to reduce law enforcement costs and increase tax revenue.

Facts

- A 2009 Rasmussen poll found that 47 percent of Californians favored legalizing and taxing marijuana, 42 percent opposed this policy, and 11 percent were undecided on the issue.

- A researcher at Carnegie Mellon University found that only 0.5 percent of prisoners nationwide are incarcerated solely for marijuana possession.

- The state of California collected $18 million in medical marijuana taxes in 2009.

- A study by Jon Gettman, a researcher who advocates marijuana legalization, estimates that America's illegal marijuana crop is worth $35.8 billion per year.

- An economist at the University of Colorado at Colorado Springs estimates that the illegal marijuana trade in El Paso County, Colorado, creates 1,100 jobs and generates nearly $30 million in income and $1.76 million in sales tax each year.

Does Medical Need Justify Legalization?

Dorothy Gibbs, 94, uses marijuana. Confined to a bed in a nursing home, she takes the drug to relieve severe pain from post-polio syndrome, a disorder that affects polio survivors years after their initial bout with the disease and whose symptoms include muscle weakness and joint pain. Describing her relationship to the drug, she states:

> I never smoked marijuana before; I had no reason to. But the relief I got was wonderful and long lasting and pretty immediate too. I didn't really have any misgivings about using marijuana; I figured it had to be better than what I'd got. They had me on lots of other medications but I couldn't stand them; they made me so sick.[67]

Gibbs is just one of the thousands of Americans who use marijuana as medicine in the 14 states where the drug has been legalized for medical use. Although not all states maintain statistics on doctors who recommend marijuana or patients who use it, numbers are available for some states. For example, as of 2008 Oregon had 2,970 doctors who recommended medical marijuana and 19,646 patients who used it; Colorado had over 500 doctors and 3,301 patients; Hawaii had 125 doctors and 4,118 patients; and Montana had 162 doctors and 1,144 patients. In California, the number of doctors was unknown, and the state had 7,359 registered patients; however, the patient registry program in California is voluntary and has not yet been developed in many jurisdictions, so that number likely represents only a small portion of the total patients. The Marijuana Policy Project, an organization that supports the legalization of marijuana, estimates that California has 190,000 medical marijuana patients.

Marijuana as Medicine

The medical properties of marijuana in both smoked and oral form have been studied for years. Most research has focused on the effects of THC, the primary mood-altering chemical in marijuana. In 1999 the Institute of Medicine (IOM), an independent research organization that advises the U.S. government on science issues, published a comprehensive review of the scientific evidence. Although the IOM report is over 10 years old, it remains the definitive and most-cited survey of the evidence on the issue. The IOM concluded that marijuana in both smoked and oral forms does have medical benefits: "The accumulated data indicate a potential therapeutic value for cannabinoid drugs [drugs derived from cannabis], particularly for symptoms such as pain relief, control of nausea and vomiting, and appetite stimulation."[68] More recently, in 2008 the American College of Physicians, a prestigious medical organization, issued a position paper updating the IOM report and advocating additional studies of the medical uses of marijuana.

The medical use for which marijuana has the most scientific support is the treatment of nausea and vomiting experienced by cancer patients who are receiving chemotherapy. Such symptoms cause extreme discomfort and can make it difficult for patients to eat and take in the nutrients they need to survive and fight their disease. Due to its effect on certain brain chemicals, marijuana is especially useful for this problem. Researchers have found that marijuana works at least as well as other antinausea and antivomiting medications and is sometimes effective for patients who have not responded to existing treatments.

In addition to quelling chemotherapy-induced nausea and vomiting, marijuana has proved effective as an appetite stimulant, especially for patients with HIV/AIDS. One of the main

"The accumulated data indicate a potential therapeutic value for cannabinoid drugs [drugs derived from cannabis], particularly for symptoms such as pain relief, control of nausea and vomiting, and appetite stimulation."[68]

— Institute of Medicine, an independent research organization that studies health issues and makes recommendations to the federal government.

Medical Marijuana: A Personal Story

While many people who use marijuana for medical purposes have dubious medical conditions, others appear genuinely to need and benefit from the drug. The story of Valerie Leveroni, featured in a 2008 book, provides an example. While a student at the University of Reno in the 1970s, Leveroni suffered a head trauma that caused her to experience as many as five seizures per day. She describes her attempts to get relief from her symptoms with traditional medications:

> The doctors tried to control the seizures with drugs . . . and nothing really worked. So the whole thing, the injury and the medications, left me feeling deeply depressed, and very impaired. . . . And the drugs made me feel so weighted down, like I was living underwater, under a veil or in a fog. Anticonvulsants are powerfully strong drugs. . . . They made me feel absolutely numb and stupid.

> Leveroni's husband read about marijuana research for seizures. Desperate for a solution, she tried it and found relief: "If I felt an aura [a precursor to a seizure] coming on, I would smoke, because I had a couple of minutes before the seizure would hit. . . . And as soon as I started using the marijuana, we immediately noted a difference in the spasms. Within weeks, we noticed a lessening of the seizure activity itself."

Quoted in Wendy Chapkis and Richard J. Webb, *Dying to Get High: Marijuana as Medicine.* New York: New York University Press, 2008, pp. 40–41.

symptoms of HIV/AIDS is wasting, the body's inability to take in nutrients it needs to maintain the functioning of its muscles and other organs. Studies have shown that marijuana increases the patient's appetite, allowing him or her to eat more food and gain weight, thus prolonging life.

Researchers have also studied the use of marijuana as a pain reliever. Some studies have shown that marijuana relieves the pain associated with HIV/AIDS and other disorders. However, many of these studies are scientifically weak. One review of the research found that marijuana was as effective as codeine but that the drug also had a depressant effect on the central nervous system of some patients, limiting its usefulness. In addition, recent studies have shown that providing the correct dose of marijuana for pain relief can be a challenge and that marijuana may actually increase pain in some patients at some doses. Based on these results, the consensus is that marijuana may be an effective pain reliever, but more research is needed to determine what illnesses it best treats and at what doses.

Medical marijuana has also been used to treat neurological disorders such as multiple sclerosis, a degenerative disease of the central nervous system. Some research has shown that marijuana can relieve muscle spasticity, pain, and tremors in some patients with multiple sclerosis, spinal cord injuries, or other traumas to the nervous system. However, like the studies on marijuana treatment of pain, these studies have had mixed results, and more research is needed.

Studies on the use of marijuana to treat glaucoma, an eye disease that can cause blindness, have proved disappointing. While marijuana does appear to decrease eye pressure, a major contributor to the disease, its effects are short-lived and require large doses of the drug. Meanwhile, other, more effective medications have been developed to treat glaucoma with fewer side effects. Therefore, the IOM, the American College of Physicians, and the American Academy of Ophthalmology have all concluded that the use of marijuana to treat glaucoma is not supported by the scientific evidence.

Adverse Effects of Marijuana as Medicine

In addition to its health benefits, marijuana poses risks to human health. Aside from its short-term effects on thinking, memory, and reaction time, marijuana may suppress the user's immune system, making it harder for the body to fight disease. This effect may be of particular concern to a person with a compromised immune

"Smoking is generally a poor way to deliver medicine. It is difficult to administer safe, regulated dosages of medicines in smoked form."[72]

— U.S. Drug Enforcement Administration, the department of the federal government responsible for enforcing the nation's drug laws.

system. However, the IOM report concluded that the immuno-suppressant effects of marijuana were not significant enough to make the drug unusable as medicine.

Long-term effects of marijuana include its harm to the lungs. Research suggests that when smoked rather than ingested orally, marijuana damages the lungs in ways similar to tobacco, causing respiratory tract infections and other problems (although studies have not yet proved that smoking marijuana causes cancer). An additional long-term risk of marijuana is dependence, although this risk appears to be relatively minor. The IOM concluded that marijuana is much less addictive than other illegal drugs, such as heroin, cocaine, methamphetamine, and benzodiazepines, the latter of which are frequently prescribed as medicine. Some long-term, chronic users of marijuana do experience withdrawal symptoms, but they are relatively mild and short-lived compared to withdrawal symptoms produced by other drugs.

Researchers have also examined the psychological effects of marijuana. Although marijuana can cause anxiety and other unpleasant feelings in some users, most people experience sedation,

The president of a cannabis industry trade school looks over marijuana plants maintained by students. Students at the school learn about marijuana laws and cultivation techniques. Businesses such as this help support the growing medical marijuana industry.

reduced anxiety, and euphoria. Some people like these sensations, while others find them undesirable. In some instances, the psychological effects of marijuana may be medically beneficial. As stated by the IOM, "AIDS wasting patients would likely benefit from a medication that simultaneously reduces anxiety, pain, and nausea while stimulating appetite."[69] The benefits of the psychoactive effects of marijuana are illustrated by the story of "Jon" (not his real name), a 37-year-old man living with HIV:

> Marijuana lifts me up past whatever symptoms I have at the moment and creates this sense of wellness and well-being that allows me to just function very much the way I could before I was HIV positive. . . . When you are really sick it affects your desire to live. If you are constantly ill for a long period of time, you can feel like it's not worth climbing back up the ladder. Because every step is a struggle. So if you can take some substance to make you feel well, even for a brief moment in time to remind you what that's like, it's invaluable.[70]

Weighing Harms and Benefits

In its assessment of the medical usefulness versus the harms of marijuana, the IOM singled out the health risks posed by smoking as the only danger that set the drug apart from other medicines. It stated, "Except for the harms associated with smoking, the adverse effects of marijuana use are within the range of effects tolerated for medication."[71] The IOM stated that due to the harms of smoking, marijuana was not recommended for long-term use. Instead, it recommended the short-term (less than six months) use of smoked marijuana for patients who met a strict list of qualifications. However, the IOM acknowledged that in some patients, such as the terminally ill or disabled, the long-term risks of smoking may be less relevant than the benefit to be gained from smoking the drug.

Ultimately, the IOM recommended further research into extracting THC and other chemicals from marijuana to be delivered to patients in a nonsmoked form. So far, two such drugs have been developed: Marinol and Cesamet. Both of these drugs contain a

synthetic form of THC and have been approved by the U.S. Food and Drug Administration for the treatment of chemotherapy-induced nausea and vomiting and to stimulate appetite in AIDS patients. The American College of Physicians recommended only the use of nonsmoked forms of THC, not smoked marijuana. It

Are California's Marijuana Dispensaries Legal?

The passage of Proposition 215 in California legalizing medical marijuana has created a legal gray area regarding the growth and sale of the drug. Since the law's passage in 1996, hundreds of stores called dispensaries have opened throughout the state to sell marijuana to patients. However, the legality of these shops is questionable. The law allows for the cultivation and possession of marijuana by a patient or the patient's primary caregiver. A "primary caregiver" is defined as the person who tends to the health, safety, or housing of the patient. In addition, the law allows patients and caregivers to establish cooperatives and collectives in which they work together to cultivate and exchange marijuana on a nonprofit basis. According to California's attorney general, Edmund G. Brown, most marijuana dispensaries do not comply with these requirements of the law:

> Although medical marijuana "dispensaries" have been operating in California for years, dispensaries, as such, are not recognized under the law. . . . The only recognized group entities are cooperatives and collectives. . . . Dispensaries that merely require patients to complete a form summarily designating the business owner as their primary caregiver—and then offering marijuana in exchange for cash "donations"—are likely unlawful.

Edmund G. Brown, "Guidelines for the Security and Non-Diversion of Marijuana Grown for Medical Use," State of California Department of Justice, August 2008. http://ag.ca.gov.

identified Sativex, an oral spray form of THC available in Canada, as well as vapor delivery systems as potentially useful drug delivery methods that should be explored for future use in the United States.

The Government's Position on Smoked Marijuana

Both opponents and proponents of legalizing marijuana for medical purposes cite the IOM report to support their views. The federal government, perhaps the staunchest critic of medical marijuana, emphasizes the IOM's conclusion that smoked marijuana is harmful and that nonsmoked forms of marijuana are preferable. Instead of allowing patients to smoke a potentially harmful and unstable plant, the federal government favors using the chemicals from the plant to develop approved medications. According to the U.S. Drug Enforcement Administration (DEA), this process allows scientists to control the potency, stability, and safety of the drugs—control that is not possible with a smoked drug: "There are no FDA-approved medications that are smoked. For one thing, smoking is generally a poor way to deliver medicine. It is difficult to administer safe, regulated dosages of medicines in smoked form."[72] The DEA compares the development of legal drugs from marijuana to the production of legal opiate medications from the opium plant:

> Morphine . . . has proven to be a medically valuable drug, but the FDA does not endorse the smoking of opium or heroin. Instead, scientists have extracted active ingredients from opium, which are sold as pharmaceutical products like morphine, codeine, hydrocodone or oxycodone. In a similar vein, the FDA has not approved smoking marijuana for medicinal purposes, but has approved the active ingredient—THC—in the form of scientifically regulated Marinol.[73]

In Defense of Medical Marijuana

Like their opponents, proponents of medical marijuana also cite the IOM report to support their position. Marijuana advocates

emphasize the fact that the IOM endorsed the short-term use of smoked marijuana and declared marijuana to be as safe as other medications. In addition, marijuana advocates dispute the claims that synthetic drugs are effective alternatives to marijuana. Activists argue that although these drugs contain THC, they lack all of the approximately 60 other active ingredients of marijuana. Therefore, they do not provide the full therapeutic benefit of smoked marijuana. As Paul Armentano of the National Organization for the Reform of Marijuana Laws states, "Marinol typically provides only limited relief to select patients, particularly when compared to natural cannabis and its cannabinoids."[74] In addition, Marinol and Cesamet are approved for a limited number of illnesses.

In response to the charge that marijuana has too many adverse side effects, advocates of legalization often explain that they turn to marijuana to escape the side effects of legal medications. An example of someone who turned to marijuana as an alternative to mainstream medicine is Marie Myung-Ok Lee, who feeds cannabis to her nine-year-old son. Writing in the *Los Angeles Times*, the author and essayist explains that her son has autism, anxiety, and digestive problems, all of which she claims are helped by marijuana. Lee reports that she turned to the drug as a safer alternative to the powerful antipsychotic medications that are typically prescribed to children with autism—drugs that the FDA has warned can cause tremors, disorders of the metabolic system, and death, especially in children. Defending her decision to treat her son with marijuana instead of these potentially harmful medications, she states: "I wouldn't be giving it to my child if I didn't think it was safe."[75]

Finally, marijuana advocates contend that the government has exaggerated the harmfulness, the addictive potential, and the difficulty of controlling the dose of smoked marijuana. They point out that many people who use medical marijuana take the drug orally (such as brewed in tea or cooked in food) rather than in smoked form. Moreover, they contend that smoking marijuana is less harmful than smoking tobacco, pointing out the lack of a proven link between smoking marijuana and cancer. In addition, they highlight marijuana's low toxicity, stressing the fact that it

"*Abundant evidence shows that marijuana is so non-toxic that, as with many medications, patients can adjust their dose easily and safely according to the relief they get.*"[76]

— Bruce Mirken, the director of communications for the Marijuana Policy Project, an organization that advocates the legalization of marijuana.

is impossible to take a lethal overdose of the drug. Finally, critics insist, contrary to the claims of the DEA, it is easy to control the dosage of marijuana safely. Bruce Mirken, the director of communications for the Marijuana Policy Project, an organization that advocates the legalization of marijuana, states: "Abundant evidence shows that marijuana is so non-toxic that, as with many medications, patients can adjust their dose easily and safely according to the relief they get."[76]

Concerns About Increased Drug Use

In addition to disputing the medical benefits of the drug, opponents and proponents disagree over the impact that legalizing medical marijuana would have on society. Opponents contend that the legalization of medical marijuana would have various negative social consequences. They argue that the effort to legalize medical marijuana is a ploy to bring about the legalization of the drug for general use. As the DEA states: "The campaign to allow marijuana to be used as medicine is a tactical maneuver in an overall strategy to completely legalize all drugs."[77]

In fact, critics contend, in the 14 states where it has been made legal, medical marijuana has created de facto legalization for recreational users. They point to California, where medical marijuana users can buy cannabis from hundreds of marijuana shops (commonly known as dispensaries) throughout the state. The law is worded vaguely enough that doctors have wide discretion regarding who qualifies for the drug. Critics contend that some doctors specialize in handing out marijuana recommendations to anyone who is willing to pay a fee. For example, Mark Borden, writing in the *Los Angeles Times Magazine*, describes getting a marijuana referral for "chronic muscle spasticity" after telling a doctor that he "occasionally experience[s] work-related anxiety, which causes muscle pain from an old back injury to flare up." Based on his research, Borden concludes, "There is a minority of doctors . . . willing to cash in on the [legal] gray area"[78] and help people obtain marijuana legally despite an absence of genuine medical need.

"The campaign to allow marijuana to be used as medicine is a tactical maneuver in an overall strategy to completely legalize all drugs."[77]

— U.S. Drug Enforcement Administration, the government agency responsible for enforcing the nation's drug laws.

In addition to potential abuse of the system, opponents also fear that legalizing medical marijuana sends a message to society—especially young people—that marijuana is acceptable, thus leading to an increase in marijuana use. Sandy Banks, a journalist for the *Los Angeles Times*, writes that in California, where the legal age for medical marijuana is 18, the law has created a more permissive attitude toward marijuana among teenagers. "Getting a cannabis card at 18 has become a rite of passage in some quarters,"[79] she writes. While Banks supports medical marijuana for the truly ill, she is concerned about the impact legalization has on young people:

> Yes, it can relieve stress, erase anxiety, help you stop worrying about why the boy you like didn't text back or how you'll do on the upcoming AP exams. But learning to manage those

A California medical marijuana dispensary technician arranges product samples. Hundreds of dispensaries have opened across the state. Critics worry that some dispensaries are supplying recreational users as well as those with medical needs.

feelings is part of growing up. Marijuana is a comfortable escape from a necessary struggle; it can too easily become a habit that saps energy and turns a motivated kid into a slacker. Yet, under the law, an 18-year-old has the same right as a 50-year-old to purchase and use marijuana legally.[80]

No Epidemic of Drug Abuse

Advocates reject the idea that legalizing marijuana for medical purposes has a negative impact on society. For example, the state of Oregon passed the Oregon Medical Marijuana Act in 1998. Since then, about 20,000 Oregonians have obtained cards allowing them to use medical marijuana. The editors of the *Eugene (OR) Register-Guard* contend that the law has not led to an increase in drug use or to complete legalization of marijuana, as opponents feared: "Ten years of experience in Oregon have shown that making marijuana available for medicinal use doesn't trigger an epidemic of drug abuse. Nor has Oregon's medical marijuana law paved the way for full legalization."[81]

Proponents of medical marijuana also dismiss the charge that legalizing the drug for medical uses will lead to an increase in marijuana use among young people. In fact, the IOM report examined this issue and concluded, "There are no convincing data to support this concern."[82] Mirken contends that the rate of teen marijuana use has actually gone down in states that have legalized the drug as medicine: "Twelve states have had medical marijuana laws in place long enough to have data on teen marijuana use from both before and after their medical marijuana laws took effect, and in every single one, teen marijuana use has gone down, not up."[83]

Striking a Balance

The arguments for and against medical marijuana reveal deeply divided perceptions on the issue. To some, medical marijuana is a Pandora's box. Once marijuana is legalized as medicine, these critics fear, the drug will gain widespread acceptance in society. As a result, full legalization of cannabis will follow, along with various social ills, including addiction, health problems, and drug abuse among young people. Others take a less pessimistic view. Any drug with mood-altering properties will be subject to abuse, they assert, but that is no reason to keep it out of the hands of those who need it in order to ease their suffering. Compassion for the sick demands that the drug be made legally available, proponents assert. Any negative social consequences of legalization will be minor, they insist, and can be resolved through responsible civic leadership.

Although he opposes the legalization of medical marijuana, William T. Breault, chair of the Main South Alliance for Public Safety in Worcester, Massachusetts, states the issue in a way that should sound reasonable to both sides: "While we strive to be a compassionate society, there must be a balance between alleviating or managing pain and creating a system that potentially does more harm than good."[84]

Facts

- According to the Marijuana Policy Project, as of 2008, 0.17 percent of the population used medical marijuana in the nine states that tracked users.

- About one-fourth of Americans live in states where medical marijuana is legal.

- According to a poll at the 2009 Minnesota State Fair, 70 percent of Minnesotans favor legalizing marijuana for medical use, while 23 percent oppose this policy change.

- A 2005 Gallop poll found that 78 percent of Americans favored legalizing medical marijuana.

- The National Cancer Society and the National Multiple Sclerosis Society oppose the use of smoked marijuana as medicine.

- Numerous religious groups support the legalization of marijuana for medical purposes, including the United Methodist Church, the Presbyterian Church, the United Church of Christ, and the Union of Reform Judaism.

Related Organizations

Americans for Safe Access (ASA)
1322 Webster St., Suite 402
Oakland, CA 94612
phone: (510) 251-1856
toll-free: (888) 929-4367
fax: (510) 251-2036
e-mail: info@safeaccessnow.org
Web site: www.safeaccessnow.org

The ASA is a nonprofit membership organization that advocates safe and legal access to marijuana for research and medical use. It works to improve access to medical cannabis by means of legislation, education, litigation, grassroots actions, advocacy, and services for patients and their caregivers.

Drug Policy Alliance (DPA) Network
70 W. Thirty-sixth St., 16th Floor
New York, NY 10018
phone: (212) 613-8020
fax: (212) 613-8021
e-mail: nyc@drugpolicy.org
Web site: www.drugpolicy.org

The DPA Network is a nonprofit organization that seeks alternatives to the war on drugs that minimize the harms of both drug use and harsh laws. It favors the liberalization of laws against marijuana for both medical and nonmedical use by adults. The DPA Network's Web site offers information on the legal status of medical marijuana.

Law Enforcement Against Prohibition (LEAP)

121 Mystic Ave.
Medford, MA 02155
phone: (781) 393-6985
fax: (781) 393-2964
e-mail: info@leap.cc
Web site: www.leap.cc

LEAP is a group of current and former law enforcement personnel who oppose the war on drugs and advocate the legalization and regulation of all drugs, including marijuana. Its members believe that legalization will reduce crime, addiction, and disease and restore the public's trust in law enforcement.

Marijuana Policy Project (MPP)

PO Box 77492, Capitol Hill
Washington, DC 20013
phone: (202) 462-5747
e-mail: info@mpp.org
Web site: www.mpp.org

The MPP is an advocacy organization that lobbies for the legalization of marijuana for both medical and nonmedical uses. It works to end criminal penalties for marijuana use by lobbying for legislation, sponsoring ballot initiatives, and lobbying Congress to reduce the federal budget for anti-marijuana ad campaigns.

National Institute on Drug Abuse (NIDA)

National Institutes of Health
6001 Executive Blvd., Room 5213
Bethesda, MD 20892-9561
phone: (301) 443-1124
e-mail: information@nida.nih.gov
Web site: www.nida.nih.gov

NIDA is the agency of the federal government responsible for supporting and conducting the nation's research into drug use and addiction in order to improve prevention, treatment, and policy. It is the sole agency authorized to approve marijuana research in the United States and to supply marijuana to be used in such research efforts.

National Organization for the Reform of Marijuana Laws (NORML)
1600 K St. NW, Suite 501
Washington, DC 20006-2832
phone: (202) 483-5500
fax: (202) 483-0057
e-mail: norml@norml.org
Web site: www.norml.org

NORML is a nonprofit organization that advocates the liberalization of the nation's marijuana laws for both medical and nonmedical use. Its Web site contains fact sheets on marijuana as well as updates on current efforts at marijuana policy reforms.

Partnership for a Drug-Free America
405 Lexington Ave., Suite 1601
New York, NY 10174
phone: (212) 922-1560
fax: (212) 922-1570
Web site: www.drugfree.org

The Partnership for a Drug-Free America is a nonprofit organization that works to help parents prevent their children from using drugs and alcohol and to find help and treatment for family and friends in trouble. Its Web site provides facts about marijuana and includes a separate section for teens.

Schaffer Library of Drug Policy
Web site: http://druglibrary.org

This Web site offers links to many documents critical of the nation's drug laws, including studies, opinion pieces, historical documents, speeches, and overviews. It contains separate sections on marijuana research, the history of marijuana, and medical marijuana.

Substance Abuse and Mental Health Services Administration (SAMHSA)
1 Choke Cherry Rd.
Rockville, MD 20857
phone: (877) 726-4727

fax: (240) 221-4292
Web site: www.samhsa.gov

SAMHSA is an agency of the U.S. Department of Health and Human Services and is responsible for programs to improve the lives of people with or at risk for mental and substance abuse disorders. Its Office of Applied Studies offers statistics on rates of marijuana use and treatment for marijuana addiction in the United States.

U.S. Drug Enforcement Administration (DEA)

Mailstop: AES
8701 Morrissette Dr.
Springfield, VA 22152
phone: (202) 307-1000
Web site: www.usdoj.gov/dea

The DEA is the agency of the federal government responsible for enforcing the nation's drug laws and regulations. It opposes the legalization of marijuana or the use of smoked marijuana as medicine. Several marijuana-related publications are available on its Web site, including "The DEA Position on Marijuana" and "'Medical' Marijuana: The Facts."

U.S. Food and Drug Administration (FDA)

10903 New Hampshire Ave.
Silver Spring, MD 20993
phone: (888) 463-6332
Web site: www.fda.gov

The FDA is the agency of the federal government responsible for regulating and ensuring the safety of the nation's food and drug supply. It holds the position that smoked marijuana is harmful and that marijuana is not an acceptable form of medication because it has not been proved safe and effective in controlled clinical trials.

For Further Research

Books

Joseph A. Califano Jr., *High Society: How Substance Abuse Ravages Society and What to Do About It*. New York: PublicAffairs, 2007.

Wendy Chapkis and Richard J. Webb, *Dying to Get High: Marijuana as Medicine*. New York: New York University Press, 2008.

David Emmett, *Understanding Street Drugs: A Handbook of Substance Misuse for Parents, Teachers and Other Professionals*. Philadelphia: J. Kingsley, 2006.

Madelon Lubin Finkel, *Truth, Lies, and Public Health: How We Are Affected When Science and Politics Collide*. Westport, CT: Praeger, 2007.

Steve Fox, Paul Armentano, and Mason Tvert, *Marijuana Is Safer: So Why Are We Driving People to Drink?* White River Junction, VT: Chelsea Green, 2009.

Rudolph J. Gerber, *Legalizing Marijuana: Drug Policy Reform and Prohibition Politics*. Westport, CT: Praeger, 2008.

Leslie L. Iverson, *The Science of Marijuana*. New York: Oxford University Press, 2008.

James Langton, *No Need for Weed: Understanding and Breaking Cannabis Dependency*. Coventry, UK: Hindsight, 2008.

Sandra Augustyn Lawton, *Drug Information for Teens: Health Tips About the Physical and Mental Effects of Substance Abuse*. Detroit, MI: Omnigraphics, 2008.

National Institute on Drug Abuse, *Marijuana: Facts for Teens*. Rockville, MD: National Institute on Drug Abuse, 2008.

Peggy J. Parks, *Drug Legalization*. San Diego: ReferencePoint, 2008.

David Sheff, *Beautiful Boy: A Father's Journey Through His Son's Addiction*. New York: Houghton Mifflin, 2008.

Periodicals

Sandy Banks, "Medical Marijuana as a Wonder Drug," *Los Angeles Times*, May 3, 2008.

Mark Borden, "High Times," *Los Angeles Times Magazine*, April 2007.

Christian Science Monitor, "Legalize Marijuana? Not So Fast," May 22, 2009.

Kevin Drum, "The Patriot's Guide to Legalizations: Have You Ever Looked at Our Marijuana Policy? I Mean, Really Looked at It?" *Mother Jones*, July/August 2009.

Sanjay Gupta, "Why I Would Vote No on Pot," *Time*, November 6, 2006.

Sarah Kershaw and Rebecca Cathart, "Reefer Madness?" *New York Times*, July 19, 2009.

Katharine Mieszkowski, "Everybody Must Get Stoned," *Salon*, March 3, 2009.

Patt Morrison, "Should We Tax Pot?" *Los Angeles Times*, December 4, 2008.

Brian O'Dea, "Lawyers, Guns and Money: 3 Reasons to End America's Policy of Prohibition," *Los Angeles Times*, June 7, 2009.

Kevin A. Sabet, "As Alcohol and Tobacco Prove, the Ultimate Cost of Legalizing Pot Is Too High," *Los Angeles Times*, June 7, 2009.

David Samuels, "Dr. Kush," *New Yorker*, July 28, 2008.

Debra J. Saunders, "Obama—Just Say No," *San Francisco Chronicle*, March 31, 2009.

Alison Stateman, "Can Marijuana Help Rescue California's Economy?" *Time*, March 13, 2009.

Maia Szalavitz, "Drugs in Portugal: Did Decriminalization Work?" *Time*, April 26, 2009.

Will Wilkinson, "I Smoke Pot, and I Like It," *Week*, April 3, 2009.

Source Notes

Introduction: Divided Opinions and Conflicting Values

1. Dan Neil, "Michael Phelps Ads Prove a New Cultural Tolerance of Marijuana," *Los Angeles Times*, July 7, 2009. www.latimes.com.

2. Jill Porter, "Phelps a Toke-ing of Pot Legalizers' Affections," *Philadelphia Daily News*, October 5, 2009, p. 7.

3. *Florence (SC) Morning News*, "Making Excuses for Sports Heroes Not Right Thing for Society to Do," February 8, 2009. www.morningnewsonline.com.

4. Quoted in U.S. House of Representatives, "Frank Introduces Bills to Prevent Federal Criminal Prosecution for Medical and Personal Marijuana Use," press release, June 19, 2009. www.house.gov.

5. Scott Haig, "Why I'm Not Against, Like, Oh Wow Man, Pot," *Time*, November 30, 2006. www.time.com.

6. Barrett Duke, "Should the U.S. Decriminalize Marijuana?" *Washington Times*, April 26, 2009, p. M10.

7. Michael Winerip, "Legalization? Now for the Hard Question," *New York Times*, May 17, 2009, p. 1(L).

Chapter One: What Are the Origins of the Marijuana Legalization Debate?

8. Madelon Lubin Finkel, *Truth, Lies, and Public Health: How We Are Affected When Science and Politics Collide*. Westport, CT: Praeger, 2007, p. 73.

9. Wendy Chapkis and Richard J. Webb, *Dying to Get High: Marijuana as Medicine*. New York: New York University Press, 2008, pp. 21–22.

10. Harry J. Anslinger, "Statement on the Marijuana Tax Act of 1937," DRCNet Online Library of Drug Policy, April/May 1937. www.druglibrary.org.

11. William C. Woodward, "Statement on the Marijuana Tax Act of 1937," DRCNet Online Library of Drug Policy, May 4, 1937. www.druglibrary.org.

12. Chapkis and Webb, *Dying to Get High*, p. 23.

13. Charles Cooper and Declan McCullagh, "America's Love-Hate History with Pot," CBS News, July 13, 2009. www.cbsnews.com.

14. Finkel, *Truth, Lies, and Public Health*, p. 76.

15. Quoted in Chapkis and Webb, *Dying to Get High*, p. 31.

16. Finkel, *Truth, Lies, and Public Health*, p. 77.

17. Janet E. Joy, Stanley J. Watson Jr., and John A. Benson Jr., eds., *Marijuana and Medicine: Assessing the Science Base*. Washington, DC: Institute of Medicine, 1999, p. 11.

18. Clarence Thomas, *Gonzales v. Raich*, FindLaw, June 6, 2005. www.findlaw.com.

19. Cooper and McCullagh, "America's Love-Hate History with Pot."

20. Quoted in Marc Benjamin, "Drug Czar: Feds Won't Support Legalized Pot," *Fresno (CA) Bee*, July 22, 2009. www.fresnobee.com.

Chapter Two: How Should Marijuana Laws Be Reformed?

21. National Organization for the Reform of Marijuana Laws, "FAQ's," March 29, 2009. http://norml.org.

22. Quoted in CNN, "Legislators Aim to Snuff Out Penalties for Pot Use," July 30, 2008. www.cnn.com.

23. Will Wilkinson, "I Smoke Pot, and I Like It," *Week*, April 3, 2009. www.theweek.com.

24. *Christian Science Monitor*, "Legalize Marijuana? Not So Fast," May 22, 2009, p. 8.

25. National Organization for the Reform of Marijuana Laws, "NORML Policy Statement," April 13, 2005. www.norml.org.

26. Marijuana Policy Project, "MPP's Vision Statement," December 1, 2008. www.mpp.org.

27. Quoted in Debra J. Saunders, "The Drug War Body Count," *Townhall*, March 16, 2009. www.townhall.com.

28. Patt Morrison, "Should We Tax Pot?" *Los Angeles Times*, December 4, 2008, p. A27.

29. *Christian Science Monitor*, "Legalize Marijuana? Not So Fast," p. 8.

30. David W. Ogden, "Memorandum for Selected United States Attorneys," U.S. Department of Justice, October 19, 2009.www.usdoj.gov.

31. White House Office of National Drug Control Policy, "Medical Marijuana: Reality Check," fact sheet, February 2007. www.whitehousedrugpolicy.gov.

32. U.S. Food and Drug Administration, "Inter-Agency Advisory Regarding Claims That Smoked Marijuana Is a Medicine," press release, April 20, 2006. www.fda.gov.

33. Quoted in Benjamin, "Drug Czar."

34. John Cooke, "The Medical Marijuana Debate CON," *Denver Post*, July 15, 2007, p. E-01.

Chapter Three: How Would Legalization Affect Society?

35. White House Office of National Drug Control Policy, *Marijuana Myths & Facts: The Truth Behind 10 Popular Misperceptions*. www.whitehousedrugpolicy.gov.

36. Mark Porter, "Cannabis and the Risks: Facts You Need to Know," *Times Online*, February 14, 2009. www.timesonline.co.uk.

37. National Institute on Drug Abuse, "NIDA Info Facts: Marijuana," June 2009. www.nida.nih.gov.

38. National Institute on Drug Abuse, "NIDA Info Facts."

39. National Institute on Drug Abuse, "NIDA Info Facts."

40. Quoted in David Crary, "Momentum Builds for Broad Debate on Legalizing Pot," *Salt Late City Deseret News*, June 15, 2009. www.deseretnews.com.

41. Rob Kampia, "3 Myths About Marijuana," *Minneapolis Star-Tribune*, May 24, 2009. www.mpp.org.

42. Quoted in Kampia, "3 Myths About Marijuana."

43. Drug Policy Alliance Network, "Myths and Facts About Marijuana," Drug Policy Alliance Network, 2009. www.drugpolicy.org.

44. Paul Armentano, "Cannabis, Mental Health and Context: The Case for Regulation," National Organization for the Reform of Marijuana Laws, May 2, 2007. www.norml.org.

45. Joe Conason, "Michael Phelps: Puppy Torturer!" *Salon*, February 6, 2009. www.salon.com.

46. George S. Yacoubian Jr., "Assessing the Relationship Between Marijuana Availability and Marijuana Use: A Legal and Sociological Comparison Between the United States and the Netherlands," *Journal of Alcohol & Drug Education*, December 2007. http://socialissues.wiseto.com.

47. Louisa Degenhardt et al., "Toward a Global View of Alcohol, Tobacco, Cannabis, and Cocaine Use: Findings from the WHO World Mental Health Surveys," *PLoS Medicine*, July 2008, p. 1,065.

48. Kevin Drum, "The Patriot's Guide to Legalizations: Have You Ever Looked at Our Marijuana Policy? I Mean, Really Looked at It?" *Mother Jones*, July/August 2009, p. 49.

49. Quoted in Crary, "Momentum Builds for Broad Debate on Legalizing Pot."

50. *Christian Science Monitor*, "Legalize Marijuana? Not So Fast," p. 8.

Chapter Four: How Would Legalization Affect the Economy?

51. Quoted in *Merced (CA) Sun-Star*, "It's Time to Talk Pot," May 20, 2009. www.mercedsunstar.com.

52. Quoted in Tom McNicol, "Is Marijuana the Answer to California's Budget Woes?" *Time*, July 24, 2009. www.time.com.

53. Quoted in Michael B. Farrell, "A Marijuana Tax as the New Revenue Stream?" *Christian Science Monitor*, May 8, 2009. www.cs monitor.com.

54. White House Office of National Drug Control Policy, "Seeing Through the Haze: The Impact of Drug Legalization in America," fact sheet, 2007. www.whitehousedrugpolicy.gov.

55. Kevin A. Sabet, "As Alcohol and Tobacco Prove, the Ultimate Cost of Legalizing Pot Is Too High," *Los Angeles Times*, June 7, 2009, p. A29.

56. Quoted in Morrison, "Should We Tax Pot?" p. A-27.

57. Sabet, "As Alcohol and Tobacco Prove, the Ultimate Cost of Legalizing Pot Is Too High," p. A29.

58. Quoted in Peter Hecht, "Oakland Pot Tax Adds Fuel to Legalization Fire," *Sacramento Bee*, August 3, 2009. www.sacbee.com.

59. Quoted in "Ammiano Proposes Bill to Tax and Regulate Marijuana," press release, California State Assembly Democratic Caucus, February 23, 2009. http://democrats.assembly.ca.gov.

60. Bruce Mirken, "Time to Regulate Marijuana," *San Francisco Bay Times*, March 26, 2009. www.mpp.org.

61. California Cannabis Initiative, "Framing the Debate," July 31, 2009. www.californiacannabisinitiative.org.

62. Tax and Regulate Cannabis California 2010, "What?" www.taxcannabis2010.org.

63. Quoted in Hecht, "Oakland Pot Tax Adds Fuel to Legalization Fire."

64. Quoted in Stu Woo, "Oakland Council Backs a Tax on Marijuana," *Wall Street Journal*, April 30, 2009. www.wsj.com.

65. Quoted in Hecht, "Oakland Pot Tax Adds Fuel to Legalization Fire."

66. *Merced (CA) Sun-Star*, "It's Time to Talk Pot."

Chapter Five: Does Medical Need Justify Legalization?

67. Quoted in Chapkis and Webb, *Dying to Get High*, p. 86.

68. Joy, Watson, and Benson, *Marijuana and Medicine*, p. 3.

69. Joy, Watson, and Benson, *Marijuana and Medicine*, p. 4.

70. Quoted in Chapkis and Webb, *Dying to Get High*, pp. 120–21.

71. Joy, Watson, and Benson, *Marijuana and Medicine*, p. 5.

72. U.S. Drug Enforcement Administration, "'Medical' Marijuana: The Facts." http://usdoj.gov.

73. U.S. Drug Enforcement Administration, "'Medical' Marijuana."

74. Paul Armentano, "Marinol vs. Natural Cannabis," National Organization for the Reform of Marijuana Laws, August 11, 2005. www.norml.org.

75. Marie Myung-Ok Lee, "Making Marijuana Legal Would Help Heal Wounds from the War on Drugs," *Los Angeles Times*, June 7, 2009, p. A29.

76. Bruce Mirken, "A Step Closer to Legalization of Medical Marijuana," *Bergen County (NJ) Record*, December 17, 2008, p. A13.

77. U.S. Drug Enforcement Administration, "Exposing the Myth of Medical Marijuana." www.justice.gov.

78. Mark Borden, "High Times," *Los Angeles Times Magazine*, April 2007, p. 144.

79. Sandy Banks, "Marijuana in the Medicine Chest," *Los Angeles Times*, April 26, 2008, p. B1.

80. Sandy Banks, "Medical Marijuana as a Wonder Drug," *Los Angeles Times*, May 3, 2008, p. B1.

81. *Eugene (OR) Register-Guard*, "Drugs and Medicine," May 2, 2009, p. A8.

82. Joy, Watson, and Benson, *Marijuana and Medicine*, p. 7.

83. Mirken, "A Step Closer to Legalization of Medical Marijuana," p. A13.

84. William T. Breault, "Medical Marijuana Bill Wrong," *Worcester (MA) Telegram and Gazette*, July 17, 2009, p. A-8.

Index

About the Author

Scott Barbour received a bachelor's degree in English and a master's degree in social work from San Diego State University. He has written and edited numerous books on social, historical, and mental health topics.